They Walked with Him

Donna VanLiere has captured the personalities of our Lord's closest followers by examining their key encounters with the Master. More than anything, this book is filled with the reality of the transformingt power of Jesus!
—DAVID JEREMIAH, AUTHOR OF *A BEND IN THE ROAD*

A good breakfast and a few of Donna's inspirational stories from her wondedrfull written book will make your ordinary day brighter and useful to the Kindgom.
—DR. KEVIN LEMAN, AUTHOR OF *THE NEW BIRTH ORDER BOOK*

This treasure of a book affords us a life-changing opportunity to walk with Christ until we discover Jesus growing inour hearts and transforming our souls.
—CAROLYN ARENDS, RECORDING ARTIST AND AUTHOR OF *LIVING THE QUESTIONS*

VanLiere paints a vivid picture of the powerful and personal impact Jesus had o "ordinary" people he called his closest friends here on earth. She recounts these well loved Bible stories in a w ay I've never seen before, and her application for us toda is both relevant and refreshing.
—CHRISTIE BARNES, EXECUTIVE DIRECTOR OF WOMENOF FAITH

If you've ever wondered whether God really uses ordinary people, your heart will at last be settled. Through beautiful word pictures and almost lyrical prose, Donn paints a poetic truth: Jesus chose them, He also chooses you…and little become much when we place all that we are and all that we have in His hands.
—MICHELLE MCKINNEY HAMMOND, AUTHOR OF *WHAT TO DO UNTIL LOVE FINDS YOU* AND *HOW TO BE BLESSED AND HIGHLY FAVORED*

Donna brings the twelve men closest to Jesus alive! At every turn of the pag you'll find yourself comforted by the fact that Jesus chose these twelve to wal with Him. And you will find yourself compelled to walk with Him too!
—DANNAH GRESH, AUTHOR OF *AND THE BRIDE WORE WHITE*

Through Donna VanLiere's artfully crafted stories, we see that God is in th business of using ordinary people in extraordinary ways.
—EDDIE CARSWELL, RECORDING ARTIST WITH THE GROUP NEWSONG

As Jesus went on
there, he saw a man
named Matthew

Stories of Those
Who Knew Him Best

booth "Follow me,"
and Matthew
follow Him

They Walked with Him

Donna VanLiere

HOWARD
PUBLISHING CO.

Our purpose at Howard Publishing is to:
- *Increase faith* in the hearts of growing Christians
- *Inspire holiness* in the lives of believers
- *Instill hope* in the hearts of struggling people everywhere
  Because He's coming again!

They Walked with Him © 2001 by Donna VanLiere
All rights reserved. Printed in the United States of America

Published by Howard Publishing Co., Inc.
3117 North 7th Street, West Monroe, Louisiana 71291-2227

01 02 03 04 05 06 07 08 09 10   10 9 8 7 6 5 4 3 2 1

Edited by Michele Buckingham
Interior design by Stephanie Denney and LinDee Loveland

Library of Congress Cataloging-in-Publication Data
VanLiere, Donna, 1966-
    They walked with Him : stories of those who knew Him best / Donna
VanLiere.
        p. cm.
    ISBN 1-58229-215-9
    1. Apostles—Biography. I. Title.
    BS2440 .V34 2001
    225.9'22—dc21

                                        2001039759

Interior art from Photos of the Holy Lands by Jack Hazut, JHM Photography.

Scripture taken from the Holy Bible, New International Version. Copyright ©
1973, 1978, 1984 International Bible Society. Used by permission of Zondervan
Bible Publishers.

For Don and Dolly VanLiere
who have been walking with Him
together for nearly sixty-two years

Contents

Acknowledgments

As always, my husband was the first to read through what started out as fragmented and disjointed stories, and he offered direction, constructive criticism, and much-needed encouragement. I couldn't work without you, *Troy*.

Time and again I turned to my old friend, *Dr. Will Marling,* for answers to all my Biblical questions. He would always answer the phone with kind words like "Donna who?" or "Aren't you finished with that book yet?" and then proceed to answer every last question I had. He even knew about the maps! His conversations always made me laugh, and then his e-mails would make me laugh again. He and Cheryl and Kate and Alex will be leaving for full-time missions work shortly, and I can only hope Ireland will appreciate them as much as I do. Thank you, Will.

Many friends, all of them gifted, read through the manuscript and provided enormous feedback and kept the stories on the right track. Thanks to *Brian Smith, Dwight Watson, Vince Wilcox,* and especially to my old college forensics buddy, *Robyn Kohlmeyer.*

Michele Buckingham's editing skills brought each story into sharper focus, and *Philis Boultinghouse* read, reread, and then read again each story and provided invaluable editorial direction. Her spirit is sweet, her smile is kind, but her pen is swift and mighty! Thank you, Philis, for the hours you gave to this book.

And finally, John Howard has assembled a staff that still cares about integrity, honesty, and character. If you met John, you would see why he so easily attracts these kinds of people—people like Denny Boultinghouse. Thank you, *John,* and many thanks to *the entire Howard staff.*

Introduction

Today their saintly images—complete with dazzling halos poised perfectly above their heads—are cast in everything from stone to bronze. Schools, churches, orphanages, and charities emblazon their names above their doorways. They are heroes of the faith, most dying martyrs' deaths for the cause of Christ. On history's pedestal they stand: loving, generous, faithful, bold, kind, and good.

Through history's faultless portrait it is difficult to fathom Saint James as ambitious, Saint John as temperamental, or Saint Peter as brash and haughty. But when Jesus chose the twelve men who would become his apostles, he didn't choose saints—perfect men living above-reproach lives. He chose twelve unexceptional men living simple, ordinary lives. Through accounts in the Bible, we see that they were often ambitious, selfish, jealous men. In other words, they were just like us!

How could Jesus use such envious, hypocritical, imperfect people? He could use them by teaching them his ways. Their school of knowledge would be a traveling classroom filled with dramatic miracles, deathbed healings, uncommon friendship, and amazing love. For three years they would walk with God in the flesh. They would touch him, eat with him, laugh with him, and learn from him. But most importantly they would be changed by him. And that is where their stories unfold.

The Bible is not specific about the disciples' emotions or feelings during the significant events of their walk with Jesus. As we read their stories in Scripture, we can only draw from our imaginations, and that is what I have attempted to do here. What were they thinking? How were they feeling? What did the miracles, the healings, the life lessons mean to them? Admittedly taking artistic liberty, I have tried to paint the extraordinary experiences of these very ordinary men in a way that illustrates that they would not, *could not* remain ordinary.

Their lives would turn the world upside down and change the course of history.

They were the apostles of Jesus Christ, and these are their life-changing journeys of following him.

Jesus went up on a mountainside and called to him those he wanted, and they came to him. He appointed twelve—designating them apostles— that they might be with him and that he might send them out to preach and to have authority to drive out demons.

Mark 3:13–15

Chapter One

Follow Me

As Jesus went on from there, he saw a man named Matthew sitting at the tax collector's booth. *"Follow me,"* he told him, and Matthew got up and followed him.

Matthew 9:9

Follow Me

It is an unusually hot morning, and the burning rays of the sun only serve to fuel the townspeople's irritable temperaments. Matthew sits at his booth on the outskirts of Capernaum, on one of the main roads from Damascus into Israel, collecting taxes from residents and tariffs from travelers passing through. So many faces go by, yet there is never a hello. Hissing "swindler" through their teeth, the people throw their money at him.

Before the noonday sun rises into position, Matthew has been berated, reviled, and spat upon by the angry taxpayers. Already frazzled and spent, he wearily begins adding up his columns.

What was it that David said in the psalms? he asks himself. *"Though your riches increase, do not set your heart on them."* Counting money and adding figures from sunup to sundown has so often left his heart aching and sore, and today is no exception. *How did David finish that psalm? "Surely you will reward each person according to what he has done."* How had he gotten into this profession anyway? As Matthew's thoughts drift, he rubs his temples, stress pulsating beneath his fingers...

He learned early on that money talks. Even as a small boy, he saw that those who have money command respect. Authorities bow to it. Kingdoms govern by it. Money makes all the difference in the world—and Matthew was determined to make plenty of it.

Mathematical equations and word problems came easily to him in school. When other students were off daydreaming, Matthew was bent over his work, fastidiously checking and double-checking his answers.

Becoming a fisherman or working in construction was never an option; he was not made for manual labor. He was meticulous, precise, conscientious, and detailed. He loved figures and statistics. And statistics showed that there was money out there to be made.

Tax gathering was a prosperous occupation, and Matthew knew that he was smart enough to do it. But this career was not without its drawbacks. Not only did tax collectors work for the Roman government, but they invariably took an extra cut for themselves. Especially hated were the Jewish tax collectors. Their kinsmen saw them as traitors—as cold-hearted, ruthless snakes. But the real snakes, Matthew reasoned, were collectors who took a larger percentage than he did. He was not as greedy as many of the others, but people still called him an "underhanded, money-grubbing scoundrel" just the same. They still considered him an outcast.

He was not welcome in Jewish synagogues, homes, or conversations. He was an astute and learned man, but there was no one who would discuss philosophy with him. No one would talk with him about the

Chapter One

> According to tradition, Matthew preached to the Jewish people in Ethiopia and Egypt. Custom maintains that he died after King Hircanus had him run through with a spear.

teachings of the great scholars. At every turn he was shunned, ignored, and snubbed. Tax collectors weren't even permitted to testify in court.

Downtrodden and weary from each day's verbal assault, he walked home alone each evening, the people's scathing words reverberating through his ears, deep into his soul:

"You're a cheat!"

"You're nothing but a thief!"

"Criminals like you should be hanged!"

The tongue-lashings had gotten so severe that each morning he questioned whether he could go back to his booth.

But money speaks *volumes*...

Pulling his thoughts back to his work, Matthew glances up momentarily and sees a few men walking toward his booth. The sun is beaming directly above them, casting their faces in deep shadows. *The one man looks like that carpenter from Nazareth. Jesus is his name,* he recalls. Jesus had always been different from the others he dealt with. He and his father, Joseph, simply paid their debt and went about their business. They were always prompt. Always polite. *Odd to see Jesus here,* Matthew thinks. *It seems he just paid his taxes.*

Even though the Jews never speak to him directly, Matthew is aware of the talk in the streets. Word is that Jesus has left his father's business and is casting out evil spirits, healing the sick, and performing miracles. Even some of the men who travel with him can cast out demons in his name. What was it that he himself had heard Jesus say one day by the lake? "The Son of Man has authority on earth to forgive sins."

Suddenly Matthew realizes he has lost his place in his count. Hunching over his work, he begins to re-add the columns. But the books and ledgers are soon masked by a dark shadow as he looks up to see the carpenter, this "Son of Man." What is it that is in those eyes? Acceptance? Friendship? Forgiveness? They look beyond Matthew—beyond his ledgers and his booth. Beyond his statistics and figures. Beyond his money stacks and bottom line.

"Follow me," Jesus says quietly.

Even his voice is different—not pinched or strained like the voices Matthew has heard throughout the day. There are no signs of hate, rancor, or loathing in his tone. "Follow me." With those words Jesus hangs a vestige of humanity around Matthew's neck that had long ago been stripped from him.

Dumbfounded, Matthew clumsily drops his books. *He wants me to follow him? He's so kind and gentle. So good. Why would he want me? People hate me!* But Jesus does not move. His eyes see past what others see—to Matthew's heart.

Matthew glances at the other men with Jesus. They are rough around the edges, a bit tattered and worn, but something is different about them as well. Then he remembers: "The Son of Man has authority on earth to forgive sins." That's it! These men are forgiven! Jesus has made the life-changing difference in them!

Money flying, pages scattering in the wind, Matthew hurriedly scrambles to the front of his booth with the freedom of a prisoner whose life sentence has just been overturned. What had not crossed his face in so many years now beams from one ear to the other. He *will* follow. He will gladly leave his hollow ambitions behind! His desire for money and the love of wealth had left him unfulfilled, unsatisfied, and unhappy. He had always known there must be something more, and now his heart explodes with the joyous realization. Into his shallow existence have come grace and acceptance!

Before given the

The book of Matthew records more about Jesus' teaching on material possessions than any other Gospel. It is fitting that this tax collector recorded the words of Jesus when he said, *"Do not store up for yourselves treasures on earth, where moth and rust destroy, and where thieves break in and steal. But store up for yourselves treasures in heaven.... For where your treasure is, there your heart will be also"* (Matthew 6:19–21).

chance to speak, his back is pounded and his hand pumped in welcoming celebration. Immediately, these men are his friends, his companions. And this Son of Man is his teacher. Matthew closes his books and follows as Jesus leads him into his new life, leaving his tax collector's booth forever behind him.

Your Walk with Him

To say that God accepts us means that he approves of us and welcomes us with open arms. He sees value in us. But in our all-too-human minds, it is hard to believe that God accepts us as we are. Surely our pasts are too appalling, our present thoughts too horrific to ever be accepted by a holy God! Some of us think, *Not me. I'm too awful. I can't even think of my past without getting sick. There are lots of people out there who get outraged when they hear my name.* Fortunately, Matthew paved the way for all of us who feel unacceptable.

Others of us may say, "My tiny sin is nothing compared to that other guy's." Matthew also paved the way for those of us who hide behind a mask of tolerability. We think, *Hey, God may not totally approve of my life, but it's good enough. I'm not a murderer, after all.* But God always knows our hearts—whether they reflect the shame of recognizing the depth of our sin or the self-righteousness of attempting to legitimize it. He knows.

Jesus knew full well what people thought of Matthew. Of all the men on earth, this tax collector didn't appear a wise choice for one of the Twelve, *his* Twelve. But Jesus saw past the job, past the comments, past the circumstances. He saw *Matthew*. Just as he sees you…just as he sees me. Regardless of what we do or who people *think* we are, God sees us and accepts us.

He's standing before us now, his eyes peering past our facades and straight into our hearts. He understands. He knows everything we've been through. With a voice that has no trace of hatred, loathing, or repugnance, he gently says, "Follow me." Whoever we are. Wherever we are. Whatever we've done. It doesn't matter; he accepts us. He values us. He sees the amazing possibilities of our future!

But do we believe that? Let's close the door of doubt, regret, and remorse over our past and simply follow. There's no need to go back into that storehouse of pain ever again. Christ has locked the door and thrown away the key.

Chapter Two

Who Is He?

That day when evening came, he said to his disciples, *"Let us go over to the other side."* Leaving the crowd behind, they took him along, just as he was, in the boat. There were also other boats with him. A furious squall came up, and the waves broke over the boat, so that it was nearly swamped. Jesus was in the stern, sleeping on a cushion. The disciples woke him and said to him, "Teacher, don't you care if we drown?"

He got up, rebuked the wind and said to the waves, *"Quiet! Be still!"* Then the wind died down and it was completely calm.

He said to his disciples, *"Why are you so afraid? Do you still have no faith?"*

They were terrified and asked each other, "Who is this? Even the wind and the waves obey him!"

Mark 4:35–41

Who Is He?

Jesus has been teaching for days now—in synagogues, in homes, on the mountainside, by the lake. On this day he has been teaching from a boat bobbing just off the shore of the Sea of Galilee. But his body is growing weary. Exhaustion is setting in. Throngs of followers have continually pressed upon him, thirsting for living water, hungering for the bread of life.

At day's end Jesus knows he must rest. But there could be no rest here among the multitude. It would be quieter and more peaceful on the other side. So Jesus, his disciples, and a few followers enter their boats and set out on the short journey. Twinkles of light soon dot the nightscape and blanket the sea with soft, illuminating reflections. The slapping of oars on water creates a rhythmic *whoosh, whoosh, whoosh* as the shoreline appears more and more distant with each row. The wind, too, is lyrical. Its cool breeze is but a quiet whisper as it gently dances across tired faces.

His eyes heavy, Jesus spots a cushion in the rear of the boat. Sleep would come quickly. He could feel it in his aching muscles.

Heaviness weighs upon the disciples' eyes, too, and their swollen feet and cramping muscles chastise them for the day's long hours. But somehow the sea air buoys their spirits, invigorating their exchange of stories as they discuss and rediscuss what they were taught today. What was it that Jesus said? The kingdom of God is like a mustard seed: It is the smallest seed in the garden; but when it grows, it becomes the largest of all the plants, its branches so big and full that birds can perch in their shade.

Suddenly, the bow rocks with unexpected turbulence as the towering sail is assaulted by an unleashed wind. Conversations halt. The disciples turn their attention to the rapidly changing elements. Before they can grab the ropes of the sail, a surging wave attacks the vessel, pummeling the disciples with stinging seawater. Lightning rips through the sky and shreds the once-proud sail. Grabbing the oars, the petrified men try to steady the heaving craft.

> The Sea of Galilee is actually a large lake located sixty miles north of Jerusalem. It is thirteen miles long and eight miles wide at its broadest point.

A violent burst from the sea snaps several oars in its fury. Their screams barely audible above the maelstrom, the disciples cling to the side of the boat. Several lose their grip and are tossed about like fish on the hull. The brewing squall hurls wave after wave into the boat. Drenched and frantic, the disciples begin to furiously bail, only to be flooded again with the sea's merciless deluge.

"We're going to capsize!"

"God, help us!"

"Where is Jesus?"

"Where is Jesus?"

"Where is Jesus?"

It finally dawns on one of the men that Jesus is still sleeping in the stern. Nestled in the safety of his Father's arms, Jesus rests comfortably. Peacefully. Though the harrowing squall threatens to swallow the boat and all aboard, his slumber is undisturbed. The terror-stricken disciples fight against the blasting winds and bombarding waves to make it to their Teacher's side. Shaking him, they scream his name above the wind's screeching howls. A weary Messiah opens his eyes to twelve distraught faces of fear and panic. Battered and bloodshot, their haggard eyes beg for answers.

Shouting above the deafening storm, they plead, "Teacher, don't you care if we drown?"

They help him to his feet. Jesus promptly scolds the wind. Turning next to the waves, he commands them to stop as well.

"Quiet! Be still," he says with a voice that is still raspy with sleep.

It is over. The murderous tempest that seconds before had threatened to consume them has been reduced to a few water drops dripping from a tattered sail and the cloaks of a ragamuffin band of disciples. The vessel once again steadies itself on calm waters.

When the Gospel writers mention the Sea of Galilee in the Bible, they often note its strong winds and sudden and violent storms (Matthew 14:24–32; Mark 4:37–39; Mark 6:47–51; John 6:18–21).

But the disciples are not calm. They are bruised. Cut. Sore. Disheveled. Their hearts still jump and throb like the waves just moments earlier. Gasping for air, some of the men lean their weakened bodies on the side of the boat. Others sit like rag dolls in the soggy seats.

"Why are you so afraid?" Jesus asks them. "Do you still have no faith?"

Why *are* they still afraid? The storm is over. Their lives have been spared.

Chapter Two

In the chilly silence one of them finally speaks.

"Who is this? Even the wind and the waves obey him!"

They knew him as Teacher. Master. Friend. But the sheer power in his voice brought the turbulent forces of nature to bow before him. The disciples had seen him open the eyes of the blind, give mobility to the crippled, heal lepers with a simple touch. But this was different. This time *their* lives were hanging on a precipice. This time it was personal! The storm had nearly drowned them all. Surely no common teacher could command furious waves into submission. No everyday healer could humble violent winds with a spoken word.

Sodden and nearly debilitated, the disciples immerse themselves in thought. The realization before them saturates their minds, flooding their hearts with the awesome, penetrating truth: The man they call Teacher, who even today was teaching them about the kingdom of God, *is God himself.*

Cold and shivering, the men silently bail out the remaining water while others pick up the salvaged oars and guide the bow toward the other side of the lake. The hush upon them is broken only by the gentle whistling of the wind, the melodic sloshing of the water, and the faint snoring of their Master and God.

Your Walk with Him

There are often times in life when we face what we think is a totally impossible situation. We crouch help-lessly in our little boats of faith, feelings of complete isolation acting as our sails as the wind beats persist-ently upon our unsteady crafts. Words like *disaster* and *crisis* thunder through our minds. In our humanness, it's much easier to panic than to see the situation from God's perspective—as a teachable moment. A time for learning and instruction.

In the mad rush of the world, it's easy to become weary and tired. The demands of work, family, and life leave us aggravated, angry, and drained. But when we're tired, our energy depleted, our minds exhausted, God's plan for our lives can seem blurry at best. We can reach a point where we can't even feel God's hand on the oars of our lives anymore—and this frightens us, and we question our relationships with God and God's relationship with us.

It is in these moments that we should completely rely on the all-sufficiency of God as the captain of our boats. But we don't. To us, it seems as if he's asleep, unaware of our problems or crises. But he is with us always, and his message to us is unchanging:

"Rely on me."

"Rest in me."

"Trust in me."

Unfortunately, when the typhoons of impossibilities grow stronger and stronger and the crises finally overwhelm us, we have difficulty *feeling* that God is with us, and our trust diminishes. We can clearly see how big the sea of problems is, but we can no longer see that God is so much *bigger*. Those mounting troubles can quickly turn us into pessimists. Just like the disciples, we begin asking ourselves, "Doesn't God care if I perish? Doesn't he care at all?"

He *does* care. He wants to do the impossible in our lives. But when problems and impossibilities sneak up on us, we start panicking, losing sight of God's hand in this teachable moment. Often it seems as if we're sailing for days, even months, alone. The wind assaults the sails of our little boats, and the waves nearly break them in two. But instead of jumping ship, we need to look to Jesus. He wants to teach us the one lesson that we can only learn in such a moment: that we are *not* alone—the master of the wind and the waves is sailing in our boats with us.

Chapter Three

Come and See!

The next day Jesus decided to leave for Galilee. Finding Philip, he said to him, *"Follow me."*

Philip, like Andrew and Peter, was from the town of Bethsaida. Philip found Nathanael and told him, "We have found the one Moses wrote about in the Law, and about whom the prophets also wrote—Jesus of Nazareth, the son of Joseph."

"Nazareth! Can anything good come from there?" Nathanael asked.

"Come and see," said Philip.

When Jesus looked up and saw a great crowd coming toward him, he said to Philip, *"Where shall we buy bread for these people to eat?"* He asked this only to test him, for he already had in mind what he was going to do.

Philip answered him, "Eight months' wages would not buy enough bread for each one to have a bite!"

Another of his disciples, Andrew, Simon Peter's brother, spoke up, "Here is a boy with five small barley loaves and two small fish, but how far will they go among so many?"

Jesus said, *"Have the people sit down."* There was plenty of grass in that place, and the men sat down, about five thousand of them. Jesus then took the loaves, gave thanks, and distributed to those who were seated as much as they wanted. He did the same with the fish.

John 1:43–46; 6:5–11

Come and See!

It is late, and Jesus is tired. He has been teaching all day. Now he simply wants to get across the sea, sit down with his disciples at the side of a beautiful mountain, take off his sandals, and rest— perhaps even close his eyes in sleep. When his boat reaches the opposite shore, he and his men plop wearily onto the ground, stretching their bodies to relieve sore, irritable knots in their muscles. Big, white, floppy clouds hang lazily above them, creeping steadily across the sky.

Settling in with his men, Jesus looks out and sees a great crowd making its way up the hillside. Word has spread quickly about his miraculous healings, and now these people have followed him to this quiet place. They clamor breathlessly up the gentle slope of the mountain, carrying their sick and crippled, supporting their aged. Some of the disciples see the crowd, too, and silently groan at the sight of the antlike multitude busily scurrying up the hillside toward them.

Although Jesus is exhausted, he is filled with compassion for the throng that is steadily pressing closer. The gnawing twinge of hunger growing angrier in his own stomach tells him that the crowd must also need a meal. Jesus looks to Philip and asks, "Where shall we buy bread for these people to eat?"

The men look quizzically at Jesus. Surely he knows they are far from a marketplace. If the crowd has not packed something to eat for the day, then they will just have to wait until they get home! But the question hangs in the air. Jesus has posed it specifically to Philip—to practical, levelheaded Philip. Jesus wants to probe his faith, to test his spiritual wings…

When Jesus first met him, Philip was skeptical. In

fact, Philip's whole life had been marked by skepticism. He needed answers to his questions about why some things worked and some didn't—and those answers needed to be based on reason, not feeling. But there was something about Jesus that made this new teacher differ-ent from the other teachers Philip had

> According to tradition, Philip preached among the provinces of Galatia and Phrygia in Asia Minor.

heard. Jesus didn't balk at Philip's questions; he didn't turn a pious ear in flippant disregard of queries that others thought silly or simpleminded. Rather, Jesus lis-tened to his questions and answered each and every one of them in a way that convinced the common-sensical Philip. So when Jesus said, "Follow me," he did. It made sense to do so.

For the first time in his life, Philip found himself groping toward something with his heart instead of with his mind. Still strictly precise, however, he care-fully told his friend Nathanael, "We have found the one Moses wrote about in the Law, and about whom the prophets also wrote—Jesus of Nazareth, the son of Joseph." To simply declare he had found the Messiah—to admit that his heart had overruled his brain—would have been too overwhelming for the practical Philip. So with painstaking thoroughness, he broke down his claim for Nathanael, as if he were still convincing himself of his discovery: He had found the one Moses wrote about in the Law—the one the prophets also wrote about—Jesus of Nazareth, the son of Joseph.

But Nathanael unwittingly knocked the wind out of Philip's not-yet-full sail. "Nazareth! Can anything good come from there?" he asked.

"Come and see," Philip responded. He knew what it was like to need answers. He understood that so many times in life, things need to be seen to be believed—and when he saw and talked

It is not certain whether Philip died a natural or a martyr's death. One custom holds that Philip was buried at Hierapolis with his two aged daughters. Another tradition holds that Philip was crucified and stoned to death.

with Jesus, he believed, albeit slowly. Cautiously. Keeping an ever-watchful eye for proof in the *pudding*...

Now Jesus asks his scientific, rational, no-nonsense apostle where they could buy food for the crowd that continues to press up the hillside. Would Philip continue to be logical and realistic, or would he abandon his caution to trust and rely on the one Moses wrote about in the Law?

The sea of bobbing heads is too staggering for the others to count, but Philip quickly tallies the number (roughly four to five thousand) and surmises the bottom line. "Eight months' wages would not buy enough bread for each one to have a bite!" he says matter-of-factly. The reality seems harsh, but there is no other way to communicate it. From a practical viewpoint, the numbers are just too many, the logistics of feeding such a crowd too incomprehensible.

Scanning the crowd, Andrew spots a young boy playing with the tail of a mangled fish sticking from his pocket. Andrew brings the bright-eyed child to Jesus, who displays the fish and a second one, along with five loaves of bread in the basket he is carrying. Jesus dispatches his men throughout the crowd, instructing them to have everyone sit. Sighing heavily, Philip does as he is commanded and sits among the followers, anxious to see Jesus "fix" this impossible situation.

After giving thanks, Jesus begins to distribute the bread—what seems to be an *endless* supply of bread! He signals to the apostles, and they jump up and laughingly hand out one piece after another to the captivated crowd. Philip, too, leaps up from the ground and bounds toward Jesus. Handing him the bread, Jesus' eyes again tell Philip, "I *am* the One." Philip dashes over the hillside, tripping, slipping, sliding as he goes. He thrusts bread into the hands of mesmerized children, awestruck women, and disbelieving men, frequently looking over his shoulder to see if the bread is still in long supply.

After everyone has eaten their fill, Jesus tells the men to gather the leftovers. *Leftovers?* Philip thinks. *Among this crowd?* His incredulous eyes cannot believe the sight of twelve whole baskets being gathered. *How could this be?* he questions. Still questioning. Still searching. Still groping. His mind races in desperation for sensible answers, for clear reasoning—for a logical explanation for what just happened. But there isn't one before him.

There is only Jesus.

Your Walk with Him

Just when we feel as if we're less of a follower because we can't wrap our minds around the awesomeness, the presence, or even the existence of God, we remember Philip. As practical as he thought he was, as sensible as others assumed he was, Philip couldn't wrap all the answers to his questions into tidy little packages with neat little bows. He couldn't even come close—because just when he thought he had something figured out, Jesus would reach into a child's pocket and pull out a miracle from heaven.

You would think that by the time of the Last Supper, Philip would have had *most* of his questions answered in a way that put his logical mind at ease. But when he requested of Jesus, "Lord, show us the Father and that will be enough for us" (John 14:8), we see that he was *still* searching, *still* struggling. He had been with Jesus for three and a half years—and he had grasped, understood, and ingested so very little. He had not thrown his caution and carefulness to the wind in complete abandonment and reliance on Christ.

Before we're too hard on Philip, however, we need to remember that his questions did show that he was still probing, still growing in his faith. He hadn't thrown up his hands and given up. He could have walked away at any time during his three and a half years with Jesus, but he didn't. He genuinely sought knowledge from the one whom Moses had written about in the Law. Still, there must have been some degree of sadness and frustration in Jesus' voice when he answered, "Don't you know me, Philip, even after I have been among you such a long time? Anyone who has seen me has seen the Father" (John 14:9).

How long do you and I have to walk with Christ

before we stop questioning, reaching, or fumbling for answers? How long before we trust completely, believe unconditionally, and rely fully in his name? How long before his presence and his promises are enough? As they were for Philip, the answers are always right before us.

Just come and see!

Chapter Four

When Storms Rage

Immediately Jesus made the disciples get into the boat and go on ahead of him to the other side, while he dismissed the crowd. After he had dismissed them, he went up on a mountainside by himself to pray. When evening came, he was there alone, but the boat was already a considerable distance from land, buffeted by the waves because the wind was against it.

During the fourth watch of the night Jesus went out to them, walking on the lake. When the disciples saw him walking on the lake, they were terrified. "It's a ghost," they said, and cried out in fear.

But Jesus immediately said to them: *"Take courage! It is I. Don't be afraid."*

"Lord, if it's you," Peter replied, "tell me to come to you on the water."

"Come," he said.

Then Peter got down out of the boat, walked on the water and came toward Jesus. But when he saw the wind, he was afraid and, beginning to sink, cried out, "Lord, save me!"

Immediately Jesus reached out his hand and caught him. *"You of little faith,"* he said, *"why did you doubt?"*

Matthew 14:22–31

When Storms Rage

Once again, Jesus is weary. Each day has seamlessly woven into a new one as he has faithfully been about his Father's work. He has been continuously teaching, healing, and performing miracles before the swelling crowds. Today has been no different.

But on this day, in addition to being weary, Jesus is grief-stricken. News has reached him that a passionate voice of righteousness has been silenced. Beheaded. The voice belonged to his own cousin and childhood playmate, John the Baptist. His heart aches as he recalls the sweet memories of himself and John running over hillsides together, their voices rising into one harmonious chorus of laughter; of swimming till they were wrinkled prunes, diving and splashing in competition to see who could catch the biggest fish with their bare hands; of talking and giggling into the night until they fell soundly asleep. The recollections pierce Jesus' heart with unending sorrow. He wishes only to withdraw to a remote place to mourn the death of his friend. How he needs to reflect and be warmed by the memories of this fallen champion of the faith. How he longs for time alone with his Father.

Jesus instructs the disciples to get into a boat and row to the other side of the sea while he makes his way to a mountainside—alone. It is here in this slight margin of time that he can find rest and renewal. Nestling his back into the soft foliage of the mountain, the wind gently lapping his face, Jesus pours out his soul to his Father. He mourns his friend. He asks his Father for direction, for help, for strength—strength to stand against the violent storm that is swirling on the horizon.

A chill sets in, the winds pick up, and cold drops of rain settle into his parched skin, washing away a day's layer of dirt and dust. It seems he has been alone no more than an hour, but already a new dawn is approaching. Thunder rolls across the skies as lightning pierces the blackness with flashes of light. The rain changes to gusty, drenching downpours as Jesus makes his way down the winding mountain path.

When the hillsides have drunk as much as they can, the heavy rainwater often swells the Sea of Galilee into a raging, unpredictable tempest. So it is on this night. The disciples have not yet made it to the other side, and as the storm's intensity grows into a frightening squall, their tiny boat is tossed and battered with every crash of the waves.

One of the disciples, straining to peer through the downpour, thinks he sees something on the water. No, it can't be. Perhaps it is the angle of the moonlight or maybe the direction of the falling rain. Perhaps he is hallucinating from the stressful day and the long hours of rowing they have put in.

But there it is again. This time several disciples see it! They squint, rub the hair and rain from their eyes, and squint again, bringing the apparition into focus. Is

Peter died a martyr's death in Rome under Nero. According to legend, he requested that he be hung upside down on the cross, considering himself unworthy to die in the same manner as his Lord.

fatigue playing tricks with their minds? No, there is definitely something out there; and with this realization they begin to scream in terror, rowing faster and faster to escape what must be a harbinger of death.

Then a voice speaks from the water: "Take courage! It is I. Don't be afraid."

It is *who?* The disciples edge up to the side of the boat, rubbing their eyes with their saturated sleeves. Is that—is that Jesus? On the water? Amazingly, the closer it gets, the more the figure looks like the Teacher.

Peter, always impulsive, always impetuous, and always intrepid, is the first to speak. Shouting above the shrieking howls of wind, he calls out, "Lord, if it's you, tell me to come to you on the water."

Peter had been born to lead, born to explore. As a child he was always king of King on the Mountain, the last to be found in Hide and Go Seek, and the first to catch someone and yell "You're it" in a game of tag. He ran the fastest, swam the farthest, and played the hardest. Someone had to be the leader of the Twelve, and he was a natural.

"Come," Jesus says with a smile.

Foolhardy and daring, Peter pushes the other disciples aside and clumsily bounds over the side of the boat. Remarkably, it is as if a solid path of earth has formed beneath his feet. Looking into the eyes of his trusted friend and teacher, he feels no fear as the others watch in amazement, clamoring for the best view. They have seen Jesus perform miracles before, but never on one of their own!

Suddenly a gust of wind assaults Peter's path, spraying stinging seawater into his eyes. His pulse races and adrenaline rushes through his veins as he realizes there is a raging sea crashing around him. The solid path beneath him begins to deteriorate. Panicking now, he starts to sink quickly, like a rock. How fitting a moniker Jesus would soon give him!

"Lord, save me!" Peter screams, swallowing a mouthful of seawater.

Had he learned nothing? When *would* he learn? Jesus reaches out, grabs Peter by the forearm, and pulls him out of the water.

"You of little faith," he says, "why did you doubt?"

Penitent and perplexed, Peter climbs back into the boat, followed by Jesus. Immediately the storm subsides.

As Peter wrings out his wet garments, the disciples begin to gather their wits. One by one the snickers begin. Slight chuckles erupt into full belly laughs as they recount how Peter flailed like one of the many fish they have pulled from these same waters. Peter, too, finally gives in to the outburst at his expense and throws his head back in hearty laughter.

But just as quickly as the laughs began, they die down as the event soaks into the consciousness of each man. The apostles quietly take their seats, exhausted from fighting the storm, humbled by the lesson of faith they have just learned. The waves are calm; the winds are quiet; the night is still and silent except for the gentle *whoosh, whoosh, whoosh* of the oars as they silently row to the other side of the sea.

Your Walk with Him

Like Peter, sometimes your faith takes you into uncharted or maybe even dangerous waters. Perhaps you move to another state. You have children. You take a new job. You face an empty nest. You experience life as a single parent. As long as you keep your eyes focused on Christ, you're able to keep your head above water. But then…*boom!* An unbridled wave capsizes your little boat of faith and drags you under. You struggle to the surface and gasp desperately for air, only to be pulled back down beneath the crashing waves.

And the thing is, you never saw the wave coming. A sudden heart attack takes a father. An infant son is buried. The cancer spreads. A teenager wrecks the car. A spouse leaves for someone else. With each crash of the waves, your pain, fright, and anger build. You've taken too many hits, suffered too many blows. You're drowning. You don't even have the energy to flail any-more. The sea has officially beaten you, and you sink to the bottom.

Throughout biblical accounts, Peter is always named first on the list of the apostles Jesus chose, reiter-ating again and again that he was the leader of the Twelve (Matt 10:2–4; Mark 3:16–19; Luke 6:14–16; Acts 1:13–14).

Peter also sank. But just when he thought the water would claim his body as its own, Jesus rescued him. So where is Jesus for us? Where is he when we sit next to our daugh-ter's hospital bed night after night? Where is he when we stare into the coffin of our twenty-year-old son? Where is he when we cry ourselves to sleep each night after our spouse deserts us? Where is Jesus when we hurt? Where is Jesus when our hearts bleed? Where is Jesus when we drown? Why doesn't he rescue *me*?

Peter faced a similar ocean of questions when, years later, he was dragged through a hostile sea of faces up a hill to his death. Life had been hard on Peter. It had imprisoned him. Broken his ribs. Bloodied his face.

Lacerated his back. Where was Jesus then? Jesus was in the water with Peter. He was in prison with Peter. Jesus was holding Peter when a cat-o'-nine-tails ripped and tore Peter's flesh. Just as he had been in the furnace with Shadrach, Meshach, and Abednego, as the Bible records in Daniel 3, Jesus was also with his disciple and friend in every trial.

And when Peter stumbled toward his own cross, Jesus was with him even then. Jesus had rescued Peter from death in the sea. And as a hostile mob dragged Peter to his cross, he finally rescued Peter from this life.

Life will beat us. It will leave us broken and gasping for air. It will drown us; it will throw us into a roaring fire. But God has promised, "I will never leave you nor forsake you" (Joshua 1:5). Dark clouds may hide him from our sight, but he's always standing right in front of us with outstretched hands saying, "Come."

"Come." What a beautiful invitation. "Come." Stated so simply. "Come." So reassuring.

So why, when we receive that invitation, do we take our eyes off our Teacher and Friend? Perhaps it is because we do not sense his presence when life's incomprehensible storms rage. But like Peter, we can be assured that when God bids us "come," when he invites us to step out of our own little boats of faith, he will always be with us in the waves; he will always protect us in the fire; and he will walk beside us when we climb that steep hill toward a cross of our own.

Chapter Five

So Little Faith

When they came to the crowd, a man approached Jesus and knelt before him. "Lord, have mercy on my son," he said. "He has seizures and is suffering greatly. He often falls into the fire or into the water. I brought him to your disciples, but they could not heal him."

"*O unbelieving and perverse generation,*" Jesus replied, "*how long shall I stay with you? How long shall I put up with you? Bring the boy here to me.*" Jesus rebuked the demon, and it came out of the boy, and he was healed from that moment.

Then the disciples came to Jesus in private and asked, "Why couldn't we drive it out?"

He replied, *"Because you have so little faith. I tell you the truth, if you have faith as small as a mustard seed, you can say to this mountain, 'Move from here to there' and it will move. Nothing will be impossible for you."*

Matthew 17:14–20

So Little Faith

Jesus has taken Peter, James, and John with him up the side of Mount Hermon, leaving the other nine apostles to continue the work he has given them: preaching in the streets and telling people about the kingdom of God. As they enter the town, word that Jesus and his disciples have arrived spreads swiftly through the marketplace, then into homes and across the countryside. One by one people make their way to where Jesus' men are, thinking that Jesus is with them—hoping to hear him speak, perhaps even witness a healing or another miracle.

Chapter Five

The growing crowd shuffles past a tiny home. The woman inside does not notice the flurry of activity. Her face is a fretwork of wrinkles—far too many for so young a face. She sits by her son's bedside, silent tears spilling off her trembling chin. They are tears of exhaustion. Of desperation. Of hopelessness. She picks up the boy's limp hand and holds it tenderly to her cheek.

Just moments before, a violent convulsion had thrown her precious son to the floor in a writhing, tangled heap. She and her husband had pinned him to the floor, restricting his flailing limbs so he wouldn't hurt himself...or them. When the seizure finally ceased, her husband tumbled out the door, dissolving into sobs. He had watched this scene far too many times...

Their son was still an infant when they first discovered he could not hear their "cootchie-coos." Deaf and dumb, he would never be able to say "Mama" and "Papa." Satan had taken possession of their beautiful treasure, his ghastly tentacles destroying their son's sweet spirit and robbing them all of the most precious moments of the boy's childhood.

Their son's sudden, violent seizures began disrupting their lives when he was a toddler. One day his mother heard a thump outside the door, then another and another in rapid succession. She threw open the door to find her son writhing and twitching, grinding his teeth, foaming at the mouth—his stiff body thumping angrily on the ground as she screamed for help. When it was over, he lay there, deathly still. With terrified eyes she looked to the towns-people gathered around them, hoping for a soft word of comfort, a gentle hand of compassion. But the villagers

The demon-possessed boy was not the apostles' first experience with evil spirits. As they traveled from town to town, they successfully cast demons out of many of the people they preached to. In Mark 6:13 we read, "They drove out many demons and anointed many sick people with oil and healed them."

only looked on in wide-eyed bewilderment and slowly, so slowly, backed away, leaving mother and son alone. Forever *alone*...

Now she kisses the boy's hand, holding it close as she rocks back and forth, back and forth. She buries her face in the child's chest and weeps over their enormous loss. There would be no father-son banquets. No sack races to cheer. No grade-school artwork to display proudly in their home. His childhood would leave only the shredded rags of suffering, pain, and loneliness hanging from the broken boughs of their hearts.

Outside, a hurrying crowd speeds past the father. As they pass, their words fall gently on his ear. "He's here," they murmur.

Who's here? he wonders.

A man and his family run down the street toward the crowd. The boy's father stops them. "Where is everyone running to?" he asks.

"We've heard Jesus is in town," they answer quickly.

Jesus. He has heard of the man who was reportedly healing lepers, making blind eyes see, and giving sound to the deaf. As he watches more and more people pass his little home, thoughts begin to swirl and eddy in his mind. Jesus. Maybe this Jesus could heal their boy. Jesus. However dim the possibility, perhaps this healer, this miracle worker, could restore their dreams and return their child to them. Jesus. He could be their last hope.

The father runs into the house and scoops the boy up in his arms.

"What are you doing?" his wife implores.

"I'm taking him to Jesus."

"Jesus? No!" she pleads, trying to pry the boy away. "Doctors and priests have never been able to help. What can a teacher do? I can't go through any more," she sobs. "I can't get my hopes up again. Just leave him here. Please, leave him here."

"Let Jesus try," he begs. "Please. Let him try."

His wife crumples to the floor, awash in tears. He runs outside, the jostling waking and frightening the boy. He pulls his son tighter and runs faster still. But when he arrives at the place where the apostles are preaching, Jesus is nowhere to be found.

"I'm looking for Jesus," he beseeches anyone who will listen. "My boy is sick."

"What's wrong with him?" Andrew asks, cupping the boy's face in his hand.

"He cannot speak or hear," the father responds. "And he often has convulsions and throws himself into fire or water."

Several apostles study the boy's expressionless face and empty eyes. They look anxiously to one another. Who among them is able to cast out such an evil spirit? Andrew is the first to try.

In John 8:44 Jesus says of Satan, *"He was a murderer from the beginning, not holding to the truth, for there is no truth in him. When he lies, he speaks his native language, for he is a liar and the father of lies."* Later, speaking again of Satan, he says, *"The thief comes only to steal and kill and destroy; I have come that they may have life, and have it to the full"* (John 10:10).

He places his hands on the boy's ears and prays that the evil that has stolen his hearing would come out. He prays passionately that sound would fill the boy's endlessly silent world. The father looks desperately to his son. The eyes are still vacant, still painfully distant. The others join their efforts with Andrew's, Simon the Zealot laying his hands on the boy's throat, praying that the mute spirit that has bound his tongue would leave him. The boy lets out a guttural, unintelligible sound in frustration.

The father's desperation grows. "Where is Jesus?" he frantically asks.

Feelings of panic set in as the remaining apostles gather around the boy, laying hands on his trembling body. They begin to pray. Feverishly. Fervently. Begging, beseeching, imploring God to heal the child—to release him from the enemy's stronghold. But the child remains speechless and deaf. The apostles' questioning eyes plead for answers. They had healed others. Why couldn't they heal this boy?

The crowd presses in on the boy and his father, craning their necks to witness an actual demon possession. Several teachers of the Law begin to argue with the apostles.

"In whose name are you attempting to heal this boy?" they demand.

"In God's name," Philip retorts.

The argument rises to a fevered pitch when Jesus—back from the mountainside with Peter, James, and John—approaches.

"What are you arguing about?" he asks his apostles.

The father pushes his way through the crowd to Jesus. "Teacher," he says, tears filling his eyes, his voice brimming with emotion, "I brought you my son..." Jesus listens to the grief-stricken father, searching his distraught face. "I asked your disciples to drive out the spirit, but they could not," the father tells him.

Jesus looks at his men. He had given his apostles authority to cast out demons at the beginning of his ministry. They had done it before. Would their faith ever mature?

"O unbelieving generation," he scolds. "How long shall I stay with you?" The apostles do not speak. "Bring the boy to me," Jesus tells the father.

Gently standing the boy on his feet, the father places his hand on the boy's shoulder and walks steadily toward the Teacher. But when the spirit inside the child sees Jesus, it throws the boy to the ground, violently convulsing and twisting his body. White foam pours from his mouth, leaving onlookers gasping and shrinking back in fear.

The apostles look to Jesus with bewilderment. Satan's hold on the boy is strong—so strong that nine of them could not cast out one demon. Could one person now drive it from the boy?

"How long has he been like this?" Jesus asks the father.

"From childhood," the father answers brokenly. "It has often thrown him into fire or water to kill him. But if you can do anything, take pity on us and help us." It is the final, desperate plea of a father whose heart has been fractured nearly beyond repair.

" 'If you can?' " Jesus replies. "Everything is possible for him who believes."

And for once in his life, the father does believe. He believes! He believes that Jesus is powerful enough to heal his son. He believes that Jesus is strong enough to pry open the savage jaws of the evil spirit that holds him. He believes that Jesus can restore his wife's laughter and song. He believes that Jesus can return his son to him. He believes, and yet…

He falls to his knees before Jesus. "I do believe! Help me overcome my unbelief!" he implores, clutching the teacher's hand.

At once Jesus rebukes the spirit living in the boy: "I command you, come out of him and never enter him again."

The boy lets out a terrifying shriek as the demon throws him to the ground. Several women scream in fright. The apostles look uneasily to one another and then to Jesus. The boy's head bounces on the ground with a sickening thud. His father kneels beside the motionless body, tears hot and blurry in his eyes.

The crowd begins to murmur and shuffle nervously. "He's dead," they whisper.

The apostles stand frozen, their hearts beating anxiously.

Jesus bends over and takes hold of the small hand on the ground. With ease the boy stands to his feet. Jesus smiles at him, and the boy's face lights up with the glowing brilliance of daybreak. In an instant the child is swallowed up in the arms of his jubilant father.

The apostles watch as the boy's head bobs out into the sea of onlookers. Why had Satan been able to consume the life of an innocent child for so many years? And why had they been so powerless to stop him? It wasn't just the despondent father who needed help to overcome his unbelief. How would they ever be able to defeat Satan alone when they couldn't defeat him together? Would they ever have the strength to combat the enemy's brutal offense?

Jesus retreats to a nearby home, and his discouraged apostles follow. "Why couldn't we drive it out?" they ask, crestfallen.

Jesus lays aside his need for rest to teach his men yet again about Satan and his power. About his brutality and cruelty, cowardice and weakness, deception and temptation. About the round-the-clock arsenal he viciously fires at his victims. Jesus tells his disciples once more that wrestling with Satan is a daily struggle that will consistently test their faith. It is a struggle Jesus experienced in the wilderness; it is a struggle they will experience in a wilderness of their own. And in that daily struggle, they will learn about the enemy's persistence, about building their faith, and about relying on the Father's never-ending source of power and strength. It is a powerful lesson that, in time, will leave the apostles forever changed.

Your Walk with Him

It was the smallest of faiths that brought the little boy's father to Jesus, a faith that believed Jesus could do what no one else had been able to do: the impossible. Perhaps when the apostles saw the boy, they viewed the situation as impossible and their faith wavered. Perhaps they were powerless because they were concentrating too much on their own efforts and not drawing on God's power and strength. Whatever the reason, their faith faltered, and they failed to cast out the evil spirit.

Our own faith wavers daily. For some it vacillates from minute to minute. What we often forget is that it's easy to get comfortable in our faith. And that's just what Satan looks for. He loves complacency, and he shrieks in delight over faith that is characterized by mediocrity. When our faith wavers or stagnates, Satan steps in. He aims for destruction, and he shoots to kill. He is expertly skilled at stealing our mental and physical health, destroying our families, robbing us of happiness. He doesn't care who we are, where we are, or how old we are. At the moment our faith struggles, he has a nose for our vulnerabilities. He worms his way into our weakness, leaving our faith crippled, our hopes battered, and our belief in shreds.

He had assaulted the father's faith time and time again. When the father approached Jesus, his faith was a tattered sail hanging from a broken mast. But there was still a small portion of that sail left, however beaten and frayed, that clung to the mast by threads. It was that threadbare portion of faith that he gave to Jesus in return for his son. He pleaded with Jesus to help his unbelief—to increase his faith. He had *some* faith but knew he needed more, and Jesus graciously added to it that day.

As he did with the little boy's father, Satan will find a vulnerable area in our lives and assault it with devastating effects. He will deftly coil his wicked, destructive claws around our jobs, our health, or our children and begin his demolition—slowly mangling and ripping apart every facet of our lives and faith. And he will attack cunningly, shrewdly, subtly every day—so subtly that we may not notice it at first. That's why Jesus stressed to the apostles that their faith was small, too small. It wasn't increasing as it should. They weren't adding to the faith they already had. They weren't building a faith that would sustain them. A faith that would combat Satan's attacks. A faith that, through God's strength, would help them do the impossible. On that day their faith was "little."

What about your faith? What about mine?

Let us cry out to Jesus like the father did: "I believe. Help me overcome my unbelief." God will surely add to our faith when we do.

Chapter Six

Take Away
the Stone

On his arrival, Jesus found that Lazarus had already been in the tomb for four days....

"Where have you laid him?" he asked.

"Come and see, Lord," they replied.

Jesus wept. Then the Jews said, "See how he loved him!"

But some of them said, "Could not he who opened the eyes of the blind man have kept this man from dying?"

Jesus, once more deeply moved, came to the tomb. It was a cave with a stone laid across the entrance. *"Take away the stone,"* he said.

"But Lord," said Martha, the sister of the dead man, "by this time there is a bad odor, for he has been there four days."

Then Jesus said, *"Did I not tell you that if you believed, you would see the glory of God?"*

So they took away the stone. Then Jesus looked up and said, *"Father, I thank you that you have heard me. I knew that you always hear me, but*

I said this for the benefit of the people standing here,
that they may believe that you sent me."

When he said this, Jesus called out in a loud voice, *"Lazarus, come out!"* The dead man came out, his hands and feet wrapped with strips of linen, and a cloth around his face.

Jesus said to them, *"Take off the grave clothes and let him go."*

John 11:17, 34–44

Take Away
the Stone

A swelling storm of opposition has been brewing against Jesus. Twice in recent days, during blistering debates, the Jewish leaders in Judea attempted to stone him. The disciples are more than relieved to shake off the dust from that region and teach on the other side of the Jordan River, just out of reach of the Jerusalem authorities.

But then unsettling news arrives from Bethany. Mary and Martha's brother, Lazarus, whom Jesus loves, is hanging over death's dark abyss. Assuming the Teacher will want to go to him, the disciples tremble at the thought of once again entering dangerous territory.

Their nerves are calmed when Jesus tells them, "This sickness will not end in death." If Jesus is not rushing to be at Lazarus's bedside, then surely the man must not be that sick.

But their assumptions are wrong. Lazarus is deathly ill. There is another reason Jesus is not rushing to be with his friend: He knows that this time, the revelation of God's glory will come in a more spectacular form than a simple deathbed healing.

The disciples go about their ministry routines for two more days. Finally Jesus announces that it is time to go back into Judea.

Go *where?*

"Teacher, only a few days ago the Jewish leaders in Judea were trying to kill you," they reason. "Are you going there *again?*"

Surely they did not hear him correctly! But Jesus assures them that they did. He explains that as long as he is walking in the light of his Father's will, he can safely enter Judea.

"Lazarus is dead," he says. "And for your sake, I am

glad I wasn't there, because this will give you another opportunity to believe in me."

Thomas, the most pessimistic, gloomy, and sullen of the disciples, knows that they have only just barely dodged one scuffle and brawl after another. If they go back, they could all be killed. Devoted to his leader yet always the morose soul, Thomas turns to the others and somberly utters, "Let's go, too, and die with Jesus."

To the Jewish leaders, the raising of Lazarus became the ultimate threat to their authority, sealing their determination to have Jesus killed.

This grim motivation resounding in their ears, the apostles devotedly follow Jesus on the day's journey back into the lion's den of Judea. Their eyes dart to each passerby, scanning the road for those who so violently oppose them. They look to Jesus, who is unwavering and unafraid in his walk. Nervously they follow behind as he leads them toward Bethany.

In the custom of the day, mourners have now been

at Mary and Martha's house since Lazarus died. Ensconced in black, the women chant laments while the men huddle together, praying in silent vigil.

Hollow and despondent, Martha wrings her hands and looks somberly out the window. It was from this same window that she used to watch Lazarus play as a child. Bounding with energy, he would rush through the door when she called him in at mealtimes, leaving it wide open for her to close behind him. After a warm, sweaty kiss on his big sister's cheek, he would chatter endlessly about his adventures of the day. "Must he always be so loud and dramatic?" she would mumble beneath her breath as she diligently set the table. "Why can't he be more serious?" Even as an adult, his childlike energy and enthusiasm continued to light up their home.

Oh, what she would give to hear Lazarus bursting through that door right now! She would stop her cooking and cleaning and sit down to listen as he rattled on about his day, his eyes sparkling and dancing. *If only his head would peek over the top of the hill,* she thinks, *and he would come bursting through the door....* But her heart knows. She will never again see his head coming over the top of that hill. She will never again hear him bounding through the door.

Nearby, another sister is slumped against an outside wall of their house, clinging to Lazarus's tunic, muttering her beloved brother's name. Mary's grief has produced only hopelessness, paralyzing her prayers. She has withdrawn into herself, into denial, refusing to let anyone sit in Lazarus's place at the table. For years he had reclined there laughing, unmercifully teasing his bashful sister till she could no longer suppress her merriment. How he loved to laugh! Her heart bleeds as she remembers Lazarus plopping onto the floor and, to the chagrin of Martha, throwing his sandals somewhat in the direction of the door. For an entire meal he would torment Mary about the handsome new fisherman in town, relentlessly teasing her until her face turned shades of sunset. Then he would laugh that melodic laugh, and ripples of delight would fill their home with all that was Lazarus. He had gotten her again! Picking up her hand, he would kiss it sweetly.

Scoundrel! She should have been angry with him, but how could she? One look in his eyes, and she would be consumed with love for her brother. Now the sandals lie empty by the door, his place at the table is vacant, and her heart is an enormous cavern of sorrow.

As Jesus and the disciples enter the outskirts of the city, a swollen-eyed Martha rushes to meet him. At the sight of her trusted friend, the grief comes tumbling from her disillusioned heart.

On Jesus' last journey into Jerusalem, he ate in the home of Mary, Martha, and Lazarus at Bethany. It was his last meal before the Last Supper.

"Lord, if you had been here, my brother would not have died."

Jesus consoles this dear big sister in her brokenness and, with a hand of comfort on her shoulder, reassures her that her brother will rise again. He gently asks to speak with Mary, and Martha goes into the house to call her sister. Mary rushes out, her shattered heart about to rupture from unbearable grief as she falls at the feet of Jesus. Her emotions flood over her cheeks, onto his feet. Here she weeps until words finally come.

"Lord, if you had been here, my brother would not have died," she sobs.

But God in his omnipresence had indeed been there and had shared in their suffering. And now his grief pours forth. Just as he had wept over the blindness of Israel as he stood on a hill overlooking Jerusalem, Jesus, touched by the pain of two sisters, now weeps freely over the death of Lazarus.

How incomprehensible. How beautifully tender. Deity is crying.

The apostles stand in reverent silence. Jesus had unflinchingly entered a hostile city in order to comfort and mourn with friends. The Twelve have learned yet another lesson today—a lesson about friendship. About love. About God's humanity. But the lesson is not over.

"Take away the stone," Jesus tells them.

The disciples stare at him in stunned silence. *Why?* Thomas thinks. *He can no longer be healed. He is dead.*

Chapter Six

Martha senses the confusion among the small crowd around the tomb. "Lord," she says, "by now the smell will be terrible. He has been dead for four days."

Jesus responds, not only to Martha, but also to his disciples who are standing near. "Didn't I tell you that you will see God's glory if you believe?"

And with that, he looks again to his disciples. The Twelve hesitantly approach the tomb. In silence they roll the stone aside. Jesus lifts his eyes toward heaven and speaks with his Father. Then, focusing his eyes on the tomb, he stretches forth his hand.

There is no movement. No shuffling of feet. A bird, seemingly uncomfortable in the quietness, suddenly flaps its wings and flies overhead. And now the voice that spoke the heavens into existence, that called the mountain ranges into formation, commands the dead to breathe again. So as not to waken all of the dead inside the tomb, Jesus calls only for his friend.

"Lazarus, come out!"

And amidst the weeping, screaming, laughing, and shouting...he does.

Your Walk with Him

The stones we roll around with us every day are awfully difficult to move, aren't they? After all, they grow heavier with each passing year.

What stone is hindering *your* relationship with God? Maybe it's bitterness, hate, jealousy, greed, lust, materialism, resentment, pride, anger, gossip, deceit, selfishness —the list can go on and on. Any of these stones can start off as a tiny pebble, but it only takes a small avalanche before it rolls and grows into a large, destructive boulder that seals off our relationship with God.

Jesus knew that the scene in Bethany was completely orchestrated by his Father's hand. Mary and Martha agonized over why God did not heal Lazarus in the way they had prayed. Why didn't he? Because God knew there was a better way. He knew that in this instance, it was better to raise a man out of a tomb than to raise him from a sickbed—just as he looks at our lives today and says, "I know this is what you want, but I've got something even better in mind."

Still, we erect giant stones in our lives—humongous

rocks that we don't want anyone to roll away, especially God. After all, they've been with us since they were teeny, tiny pebbles, and we are quite used to them now.

Jesus knew that Lazarus had to be dead for a few days before his disciples would take away their own stones and believe in him. Thomas's stone, no doubt, was pessimism. For James, it was perhaps ambition or personal gain. Judas Iscariot's stone could have been resentment or jealousy. Whatever the disciples were clinging to, it was obstructing their communion with Christ. Yes, they followed him. Yes, they loved him and were willing to die with him in Judea if need be. But they were also holding on to those destructive stones.

Jesus knew they'd experience something better than they'd ever imagined if they would just remove their stones! "Take away the stone," he said. And when they did, new life appeared—not only for Lazarus, but for all those who believed.

"Take away the stone," Jesus says to us today. He knows that new life—better than anything we could imagine—is waiting just beyond that stone. Do we believe him enough to move it?

Chapter Seven

He Brought Them to Jesus

The next day John was there again with two of his disciples. When he saw Jesus passing by, he said, "Look, the Lamb of God!"

When the two disciples heard him say this, they followed Jesus. Turning around, Jesus saw them following and asked, *"What do you want?"*

They said, "Rabbi" (which means Teacher), "where are you staying?"

"Come," he replied, *"and you will see."*

So they went and saw where he was staying and spent that day with him. It was about the tenth hour.

Andrew, Simon Peter's brother, was one of the two who heard what John had said and who had followed Jesus. The first thing Andrew did was to find his brother Simon and tell him, "We have found the Messiah" (that is, the Christ). And he brought him to Jesus....

The great crowd that had come for the Feast heard that Jesus was on his way to Jerusalem.

They took palm branches and went out to meet him, shouting, "Hosanna!"…

Now there were some Greeks among those who went up to worship at the Feast. They came to Philip, who was from Bethsaida in Galilee, with a request. "Sir," they said, "we would like to see Jesus." Philip went to tell Andrew; Andrew and Philip in turn told Jesus.

John 1:35–42; 12:12–13, 20–22

He Brought
Them to Jesus

A great crowd has come
into the city for the Feast of the Passover and has heard
that Jesus is making his way into town. Waving palm
branches in the air, the sea of spectators lines the city
route, hoping for a glimpse of the Messiah.
Anticipation swirls as a child on his father's shoulders
cries out. He has spotted Jesus, seated on the back of a
donkey, slowly making his way through the overrun
streets.

Jostled about by the crowd, a spark ignites in the
belly of each apostle, setting their nerves on high alert
as they cautiously elbow their way through the squeeze

of onlookers. *Are these people followers of Jesus or part of a plot instigated by the Pharisees to capture him?* the apostles wonder. But their fears subside as the masses begin to shout.

"Hosanna!"

"Blessed is he who comes in the name of the Lord!"

"Blessed is the King of Israel!"

The people pressing in on them are not enemies but believers! Housewives. Merchants. Teachers. Students. All have come to look at Jesus. To touch him. Hear him. Speak with him. The apostles attempt to maintain some sense of control as the horde in the bloating roadway presses in around them.

Philip, on the outside of the activity circling Jesus, feels a hand on his shoulder. Turning, he is greeted not by one of the other disciples or a Jewish brother or sister but by a small group of Gentiles, Greeks who have traveled to Jerusalem for the feast.

"Sir," they say cordially, "we would like to see Jesus."

Philip hesitates before responding. Don't these Gentiles see how many Jewish people are here to see

Jesus? Don't they know that from its inception, the ministry of Jesus has been first to the Jews? Puzzled about what to do, Philip looks around for one of the other disciples. Some distance away he sees Peter, James, and John, all busy in conversation. Standing on his toes, he cranes his neck to see through the mob and spots Andrew leaning over and laughing with a small boy. *Perhaps Andrew will know what to do.*

"Follow me," Philip says as he leads the men through the masses.

According to tradition, after Christ's resurrection Andrew preached in the province of Achaea in Greece. He died a martyr's death on an X-shaped cross. Centuries after his death, Andrew's remains were being taken to Scotland when the boat carrying them shipwrecked in a bay—later named St. Andrew's Bay.

Rugged Andrew, down on one knee in front of a tot no older than five, pretends to pull a coin from the enthused child's ear. A squeal of delight filters through the noise of the streets as the boy's face sparkles with newfound wonder at what had been hiding in his ear. Andrew's large, muscular frame bounces with laughter along with his tiny new friend's. When he looks up, he sees Philip approaching with a group of foreigners. Philip has no time to introduce them, for the warm, amiable, smiling Andrew is already shaking hands, already learning names.

At ease, the Gentiles tell Andrew that they would like to see Jesus. Andrew's soul stirs as he reflects on the words Jesus had spoken not long before: "Many will come from east and west and will take their places at the feast in the kingdom of heaven." There is no reason to hesitate. Of course he will take them to Jesus!

It had been only a few years earlier when Andrew had taken his own brother, Peter, to meet the Messiah…

The brothers had worked together in the family business since they were young boys. Growing up, Andrew had often marveled at his brother's prowess on the boat, pulling bulging nets from the waters along with men twice his size. Peter was a robust, headstrong youth who grew into a burly, hardworking, determined adult. When he was old enough, he naturally took the reins of the business, with Andrew as second in charge.

But living in the shadow of his big brother was not burdensome for the quiet, unassuming Andrew. Steadfast, reliable, the family's peacemaker, he preferred having Peter in charge of the financial and logistic aspects of the business while he focused on the day-to-day tasks of maintaining equipment and supplies. In return, the quick-tempered and stubborn Peter gladly placed his diplomatic brother over the hired hands. To their fishing crew, the calm, mild-mannered Andrew was a peace in the eye of Peter's frequent storms.

Then one day, friends of Andrew told him of a fiery young preacher named John the Baptist who was baptizing people in the Jordan River. The unrestrained proclaimer called it "a baptism of repentance for the forgiveness of sins."

Anxious to hear this radical crusader for himself, Andrew traveled the one hundred-plus miles south from Bethsaida to Bethany near the Jordan River.

Here he found the odd-looking, charismatic preacher. "Make straight the way for the Lord!" he urged his followers. To the cynical, questioning Pharisees, he blasted: "He is the one who comes after me, the thongs of whose sandals I am not worthy to untie!" Intently listening, Andrew grappled with questions of his own. Could the man of whom John spoke be the promised Messiah? A devout student of the Old Testament and stalwart in his quest to gain knowledge of the Lord, Andrew absorbed each word John taught about the Son of God.

Then one day another man passed by the river. John exclaimed, "Look, the Lamb of God!" *Is this the Messiah?* Andrew wondered. He and another of John's disciples turned and followed tentatively behind Jesus, searching for the right words, the right moment to say something.

"What do you want?" Jesus asked, turning to them.

Could this possibly be the Son of God? He looks so...commonplace. As Andrew studied Jesus' face, the eyes that had witnessed the glory of Creation permeated the far reaches of Andrew's soul, unfurling an indescribable peace in his heart. Unable to verbalize something more profound, Andrew finally stumbled, "Rabbi, where are you staying?"

"Come," Jesus invited, "and you will see."

So sweet and simple. It was an invitation of cleansing. Of friendship. Of redemption. However brief, a moment like this has a way of standing time on end. The words seemed to hang endlessly, a suspended rainbow of hope above Andrew. "Come, and you will see." Like one of the many cormorants that often swooped down to snatch a fish from their boat, Andrew hungrily seized the invitation and spent the next many hours with Jesus. By day's end, there were no questions in his mind. Jesus *was* the Son of God. The promised Messiah.

Andrew hurried home with one thought on his mind: *Peter.* All Andrew's life, Peter's gregarious personality had easily dwarfed his own. Peter was bigger. Stronger. More popular. More outgoing. Much more aggressive. Yet humble Andrew didn't see their differences as vices, but gifts—gifts both men could use now as followers of Jesus.

With irrepressible joy he traveled back to the shores of Galilee. He spotted his big brother in the distance busily cleaning nets, the warm Mediterranean sun turning his ruddy complexion a shade of burnt copper.

"Peter!" Andrew shouted victoriously.

Wiping the sweat from his face, Peter looked up from his work, smiling at the return of his little brother. Breathless, Andrew grabbed Peter by the shoulders, locking eyes with him. Aware of Peter's somewhat skeptical nature, Andrew knew that his brother would turn a deaf ear to him unless he expressed 100 percent certainty about what he had discovered.

"We have found the Messiah!" he said steadily. There was no doubt, hesitation, or indecision in his voice.

Andrew is mentioned three times in the Gospels, and all three times he is bringing someone to Jesus: first his brother, Peter; then the group of Gentiles; and later, as John 6:8–9 records, a little boy whose two fish and five barley loaves Jesus would use miraculously to feed five thousand people.

Peter knew better than to question his brother's earnestness. Working side by side with Andrew for so many years had given him a deep and abiding respect for his little brother. Peter dropped his work and left his nets, his boat, and his business behind and simply followed as Andrew led him to *Jesus*...

Now, three and a half years later, Andrew makes his way through the bustling streets of Jerusalem, leading a group of searching Gentiles to meet the Savior, Jesus. Peter, busy preparing for the remainder of the day, catches the activity out of the corner of his eye and smiles. Once again, his faithful, steadfast brother is humbly leading others to Christ.

Your Walk with Him

History never remembers the Andrews of this world. It is the Peters who go down as heroes. The Andrews can't perform in front of thousands, preach vibrant sermons, or lead a crusade. What they can do, and do well, is reach out with great humility and love to *one person at a time.* Behind each of the world's great theologians, authors, singers, and evangelists stands an Andrew—a behind-the-scenes someone who took each of these great men and women by the hand and introduced them to Christ.

Andrew was the first disciple to follow Jesus. In the leadership ranks, however, he quickly took a backseat to Peter, James, and John. But there are no indications in the Bible that he was sour, cynical, or bitter about his position within the group because he found Jesus first. There would have been no Peter without Andrew. Yes, Peter preached to thousands, but it was Andrew who brought people one by one to hear him. The Andrews of the world generally have one single, beautiful gift: a passion to personally tell others, "We have found the Messiah!"

Too often we look at someone else's life and say, "I can't sing like she can" or "I'm not charismatic and charming like he is." We have a tendency to look at that person's enormous gifts and talents and compare them to our own—and we always seem to come up short. But so often, the ones in the spotlight aren't the ones gifted in personal, one-on-one communication. Perhaps we, like Andrew, have the ability to make people feel loved and at ease. Perhaps we have a way of making them feel important by the words we say; by the cards and letters we send; by our actions around the office, in school, or at home. Perhaps we bear that irrepressible quality that makes them want to know more about our Messiah.

That's just how God's love spreads—one heart at a time. In God's master plan, nothing could have been done without Andrew; and today, nothing can be done without you and me. We can't all have leadership talents like Peter, but we can all be more like Andrew. And the ability to love others is the greatest gift of all!

Chapter Eight

Love Held Him There

Then came the day of Unleavened Bread on which the Passover lamb had to be sacrificed. Jesus sent Peter and John, saying, *"Go and make preparations for us to eat the Passover."* ...

They left and found things just as Jesus had told them. So they prepared the Passover. ...

And he took bread, gave thanks and broke it, and gave it to them, saying, *"This is my body given for you; do this in remembrance of me."*

In the same way, after the supper he took the cup, saying, *"This cup is the new covenant in my blood, which is poured out for you. But the hand of him who is going to betray me is with mine on the table. The Son of Man will go as it has been decreed, but woe to that man who betrays him."* They began to question among themselves which of them it might be who would do this.

Also a dispute arose among them as to which of them was considered to be greatest.

They went to a place called Gethsemane, and Jesus said to his disciples, *"Sit here while I pray."* He took Peter, James and John along with him, and he began to be deeply distressed and troubled. *"My soul is overwhelmed with sorrow to the point of death,"* he said to them. *"Stay here and keep watch."*

Luke 22:7–8, 13, 19–24; Mark 14:32–34

Love Held Him There

The *streets* *of Jerusalem* are swollen with religious pilgrims who have come in anticipation of the Passover feast, celebrating God's deliverance of the Jews from Egypt. Jesus and his men also plan to share the Passover meal together.

"Go on ahead of us into the city and make preparations for the evening," Jesus charges Peter and John. So the two men walk boldly into town to prepare the table for the Son of God's Passover meal—unaware that in a few short hours, he would be their Passover Lamb.

As the aroma of lamb and bitter herbs fills the

room, the apostles arrive and quickly take their seats. They are tired and hungry and ready for this, the most sacred of Jewish feasts. Around the table they share with Jesus the wine and bread that he offers in his remembrance, and they speak of the many healings, blessings, and miracles they've witnessed in recent days. They laugh as they recall the more whimsical events in their travels together, each story a perfectly crafted gem of humor blending both fact and fiction and aimed at ribbing one another. They are still chuckling as Jesus begins to speak. "This very night you will all fall away on account of me, for it is written: 'I will strike the shepherd, and the sheep of the flock will be scattered.'"

Their gaiety ends abruptly. Each apostle strikes an immutable stance. What a preposterous accusation! At rapid-fire pace they cry out their innocence.

"Not I!"

"I would never!"

"You know my heart, Lord!"

Their grand exclamations quickly turn competitive, heating into a fevered argument: Which man is the most righteous, the most loyal—and therefore the most deserving of a position in the upper echelon of the kingdom?

John, sitting next to Jesus, feels the heat of anger mounting within him. Although his quick temper has been tamed from years of following Jesus, he once again feels his former nature erupting—that thundercloud about to burst—as he jockeys along with the rest for top position. (There was a *reason* Jesus nicknamed John and his brother, James, the "sons of thunder"!) Wasn't it just yesterday that he and James had asked, at their mother's urging, to be given seats of honor on Christ's left and right

The closeness of John's relationship to Jesus was illustrated at the crucifixion when Jesus, speaking from the cross, charged John to look after his mother, Mary: "When Jesus saw his mother there, and the disciple whom he loved standing nearby, he said to his mother, *'Dear woman, here is your son,'* and to the disciple, *'Here is your mother.'* From that time on, this disciple took her into his home" (John 19:26–27).

in the kingdom? Born to a status-seeking mother, ambition is unquestionably in John's genes. But for three and a half years now, Jesus has been growing in his heart.

Reining in his anger, John throws off the lies of power, materialism, significance, and position and quells the voices that have grown into a cacophonic din. No wonder Jesus loves him so! Of all the disciples, John has the greatest capacity to understand…to feel…to love.

He hasn't always been this way. Spending time with Jesus has transformed his soul.

Their argument calmed, the men take their seats again as Judas slips quietly into the night. The door closes behind him as the night chill sets in, the last flickers of sunlight extinguished by raven-colored darkness. The Passover meal comes to an end.

Jesus rises and his disciples accompany him to the garden of Gethsemane, a peaceful, uninhabited place that is his favorite spot to talk with his Father. Tired and full, they closely follow Jesus through the silent streets, over a rocky embankment, and into the lush Valley of Kidron. A grove of olive trees stands just beyond them, and Jesus leads his weary band to its edge. Jesus seems unusually quiet and preoccupied this evening, but they assume that their Teacher is simply tired after a long day.

A strange sadness in his voice, Jesus asks John, Peter, and James to keep watch while he prays. *At this hour?* John wonders. *Keep watch? For what?* Finding soft ground, the three sit, bracing their backs against large olive trees, while Jesus goes deeper into the garden. A whispering breeze caresses the leaves above them as a sliver of moonlight peeks through. One by one, their stomachs satisfied and the night weighing heavily on their eyes, each man gives in to slumber.

Jesus finds them this way not once but three times. His third time to wake them would be his last.

"Are you still sleeping and resting?" he says. "Enough! The hour has come. Look, the Son of Man is betrayed into the hands of sinners." Wearily, John lifts his head to catch glimpses of light moving toward them through the trees. Jumping to his feet, his eyes dart to his left and right as an angry mob surrounds them. Peter and James are also on their feet, heads turning, bodies spinning, like animals ready for the slaughter. But it is not the sheep these executioners are after. It is their Shepherd.

The incensed faces render John speechless and unable to move. Fright turns into disbelief as he spots a sheep among this savage pack of wolves. What is Judas doing here? With *them?* A kiss to the cheek arouses blood-thirsty snarls from the salivating wolves. Stunned, John remains catatonic as ferocious howls pierce the air. His paralyzed legs wobble backward as the beasts seize the Good Shepherd and savagely drag their prey away.

After his abandonment of Jesus in the garden, John was given a tremendous "do over" and went on to live one of the greatest lives in history. He died a natural death in Ephesus—the last of the apostles to die.

Running frantically into the shadows, John panics each time he stumbles into a tree, his speeding heart pounding in his ears, his earlier bravado reduced to common fear and self-preservation. Awakened from sleep, a disgruntled bird flies from its nest. John turns at the sound, prepared to fight. Recognizing his "enemy," his body goes limp. He doubles over, holding his ribs as he gasps for air. Tears of fright fill his eyes, spilling into his shaking hands. A wave of nausea hits him. His weakened body convulses as his fear regurgitates onto the dew-soaked ground.

Drenched with sweat, he recalls how Jesus' body had dripped with perspiration in the garden. And he remembers the words he'd heard Jesus pray before he fell asleep. How passionately Jesus had prayed! How his voice had broken with emotion as he reached out to his Father and begged that this dreaded cup be taken from him!

He wanted John to come with him that night because he needed his friendship. His prayers. His love. His support. It was the hour of Jesus' greatest need, and all he asked of John was that he stay awake and pray. But John did neither. He gave him nothing.

Broken and crying now, John knows in his heart that Jesus has already forgiven him. But how can he ever forgive himself? These agonizing thoughts are more than he can bear. He does not linger in this place long.

A dim string of lights flicker in the distance as John, lagging safely behind, cautiously follows the mob that holds Jesus in custody. His family's association with the high priest provides his entrance into the temple court-yard, where he witnesses the trial of his Lord.

By morning, the streets are crackling with curiosity. Word of Jesus' capture has spread, and people have lined up to catch a glimpse of this infamous Jewish out-law on his way to execution. It is through this caustic crowd that John ushers his own mother and Mary, the mother of Jesus, to Golgotha. Both women bury their faces into John's chest as he—boldly now and with fierce courage—walks through the midst of the mob.

He had deserted Jesus last night. He would not do it again.

With each swing of the soldier's hammer, cries and cheers erupt from those gathered on the hill. Jesus does not utter a harsh word. John stands resolutely as some in the crowd recognize him and begin to taunt him, spitting on him and grabbing his clothing. "Why don't you run away like the others?" they mock. His resolve intensifies. He would not run again.

The cross is hoisted into place then dropped into the earth with a resounding thud as Jesus' tortured, flogged, and lacerated body is raised into view. The gathering throng shouts with delight. His followers, weak with emotion, fall to their knees. John stands tall.

In his weakness, he had fallen last night. He would not fall again.

Smelling blood in the air, the sneering jackals bare their teeth.

"If you are the Son of God, come down from that cross!"

"Where is your God now?"

But John knows it is not God who keeps Jesus on that cross. It is *love* that holds him there. Love for each of them. Love for his Father. Love for *him*.

And it is love that holds John here.

Your Walk with Him

The reality of our humanity can be so discouraging. Wouldn't it be great to say that we always walk honorably and uprightly before God and people? That we never bring disappointment or shame to the cause of Christ?

But the truth is, we blow it. Most of us, on a daily basis. We let little things build up till we feel that familiar thunder rolling inside. We get a little snippy with that bank teller who is as slow as Christmas. We want to choke the cashier at the grocery store for closing the drawer *again* before giving us change, making us wait even *longer* while she calls a manager to open it. We screen our calls so we won't have to talk to so-and-so. We yell at our kids for no particular reason. We argue with our spouse and walk away mad. We get annoyed with our parents and refuse to call or speak to them for several weeks. Like John and his brother, James, we definitely qualify as children of thunder!

Remember playing childhood games? Nobody ever paid any attention to proper rules or regulations. If something didn't play out right, someone would yell, "Do over!" Well, with God, every day is a do-over day. We can beat our chest and moan and scream at ourselves all we want, but God has already said, "Do over!" One of the greatest challenges in our daily walk is accepting God's forgiveness. What is it inside us that wants to *cling* to our sins? If we have genuinely asked for forgiveness, then we've got it. Now we need to forgive ourselves.

This isn't to say that we can keep on doing what we have been doing, taking advantage of God's forgiveness. Like John, we have to grow out of our old ways and into new ones. And only we know what those "old ways" are. We know what trappings of the world take our eyes off Christ. We know what snares entangle us. We know which sins we fall into time and time again.

And sometimes, like John, we blow it big. When that happens, like John, we must get back up and keep walking, keep following, keep seeking.

Then, when we fall, we can turn our ear to heaven and listen for that voice from above that gently whispers, "Do over!"

Chapter Nine

The Denial

Then Simon Peter, who had a sword, drew it and struck the high priest's servant, cutting off his right ear. (The servant's name was Malchus.)

Jesus commanded Peter, *"Put your sword away! Shall I not drink the cup the Father has given me?"*

Then seizing him, they led him away and took him into the house of the high priest. Peter followed at a distance. But when they had kindled a fire in the middle of the courtyard and had sat down together, Peter sat down with them. A servant girl saw him seated there in the firelight. She looked closely at him and said, "This man was with him."

But he denied it. "Woman, I don't know him," he said.

A little later someone else saw him and said, "You also are one of them."

"Man, I am not!" Peter replied.

About an hour later another asserted, "Certainly this fellow was with him, for he is a Galilean."

Peter replied, "Man, I don't know what you're talking about!" Just as he was speaking, the rooster crowed. The Lord turned and looked straight at Peter. Then Peter remembered the word the Lord had spoken to him: *"Before the rooster crows today, you will disown me three times."* And he went outside and wept bitterly.

John 18:10–11; Luke 22:54–62

The Denial

$\mathcal{E}$*ven at this late* hour, a squawking crowd circles the gates of the high priest's house
like ravenous birds of prey. Peter, head bent low, keeps
to himself, blending in with the carrion vultures who
are hungry for word of the trial. Rubbing his hands
together, he shoves chilled fingers under his arms and
nervously walks past the gate.

His nerves frayed, the night air stinging his lungs,
Peter contemplates his next move. Perhaps he could
track down the other men and together they could
fight their way into the house. Steadying himself, he

decides against this, his stomach still churning from the terrifying moment in the garden just a few hours earlier…

Several armed militants seized Jesus as Peter, wild with horror, wielded his sword and deftly lobbed off a soldier's ear. Cries of anguish erupted as blood spurted from the gaping wound. The angry squadron reached for their weapons.

"Put your sword away!" Jesus rebuked Peter. "Shall I not drink the cup the Father has given me?"

Blood oozed between the guard's shaking fingers; but with one touch, Jesus restored the ear. What irony! Not long ago Jesus had said, "He who has ears, let him hear." This man's ear had miraculously been healed in front of hundreds of his comrades, yet still their ears were closed.

They swept in, clamping their talons firmly into Jesus' flesh as Peter, struck cold with fear, ran blindly into the olive grove—his love for Jesus so easily *dislodged*…

The Denial

The hovering crowd outside the high priest's house presses upon the gate, and a servant finally swings it open. Peter pushes his way into the courtyard unnoticed. Covering much of his face, he breathes hot air into his hands as he glances about the grounds. Casting bets on the fate of Jesus, curious spectators lurch around the courtyard—perching on benches, squawking in groups, nesting atop the stairs.

Loud crackles of fire beckon Peter's attention, the flames licking high

On the night of his arrest, Jesus encouraged Peter with these words: *"Simon, Simon, Satan has asked to sift you as wheat. But I have prayed for you, Simon, that your faith may not fail. And when you have turned back, strengthen your brothers"* (Luke 22:31–32). Though Peter's failure on the night of Jesus' arrest was monumental in history, it did not cripple him as Satan had hoped. After Jesus' resurrection, "the Rock" returned to his role as leader of the apostles, ultimately leading them in the founding of the New Testament church.

into the night air. Maybe he could think more clearly if he were warmer. Kneeling before the blood-orange heat, he watches as a twig, crusted gray with ash, plummets into the fire, heaving a brilliant flurry of orange sparks into his face. Sitting here, he will be able to devise a plan to rescue Jesus. The covey around the fire cackles about death for Jesus, their pinched voices rising into one unified shriek.

Peering through the flames, a servant girl squints at the quiet, hollow-eyed stranger across from her. "This man was with him," she caws knowingly.

Peter's heart jumps. His head jerks up to the piercing stares. Flush with heat, his hairs on end, sweat stands cold on his forehead as he calmly denies the accusation.

"Woman, I don't know him."

Embarrassed by his gaze, the servant casts her eyes back to the fire. Once he senses that she and the others are satisfied, Peter slips away toward a darkened corner of the courtyard. What good would it do to get into a brawl with so many who clearly oppose Jesus?

The Denial

There has been enough trouble for one night. Tightening his robe around him, Peter keeps his head down as he passes a large, menacing guard. The soldier had heard the slight commotion at the fire and is keeping a watchful eye on Peter. "You also are one of them," he alleges.

"Man, I am not," Peter replies brusquely as he hurriedly passes.

It is not safe here. How can he help Jesus when his own life is so obviously in danger? His heart racing, he feels trapped in this shrinking space—crowded with the enemy's hatred and his own welling fear. Finally he finds a solitary space in the dark. He stops and wipes the sweat from his face and neck. Earlier in the evening he had been so bold and strong. So rock-steady. "Lord, I am ready to go with you to prison and to death," he had staunchly told Jesus. Now he is frightened. Panic-stricken. Weak. Shivering nervously in the shadows.

To avoid standing out, Peter skirts the outside of one group then shuffles to another. From where he is stationed, he can make out part of Jesus' profile inside the chief priest's quarters. Each group hisses death for Jesus. "They should kill him and his men as well," an elderly man screeches.

Peter's knees weaken as he begins to shrink away.

Catching Peter's hesitant movement, a young man studies his face and steps toward him. "Certainly *this* fellow was with him, for he is a Galilean," he cackles accusingly.

Fire burns in Peter's belly. Blood rushes to his head. He hotly denies the accusation. Vehemently swearing and cursing, he spits out, "Man, I don't know what you're talking about!" The accuser resigns himself to a group standing nearby and turns his attention to their conversation.

God still worked through Peter despite his incredible failure—despite his many flaws—as evidenced in Acts 5:15: "As a result, people brought the sick into the streets and laid them on beds and mats, so that at least Peter's shadow might fall on some of them as he passed by." God's power was so strong in Peter's life that even people who passed through his shadow were healed.

Peter is once again free.

But in the distance, he hears it. A rooster stretches long its neck…spreads its wings…and crows.

He cannot breathe. The words of Jesus choke the air from his chest, dousing his heart and soul with chilling truth: "Before the rooster crows today, you will disown me three times."

Horror-stricken, Peter snaps his head toward the house; he clearly sees Jesus standing at the top of the stairs looking at him. However, the look is not one of rebuke but of sorrow. And beyond the sorrow, Peter sees love…and compassion. He perceives not judgment but forgiveness. It is a look that only a father can give his child. However brief, the moment is more than Peter can take. Devastated, he runs out into the street and weeps uncontrollably, painful tears blinding his eyes. Agonizing feelings of guilt explode from his lungs as "the Rock" crumbles to his knees.

"Forgive me…forgive me," he whispers between tortured sobs. "Oh Jesus, forgive me."

Staggering to his feet, his cries rising above the noise of the courtyard, he runs aimlessly through the streets toward a horizon of imminent death for his Lord and Friend.

Your Walk with Him

As we grow older, we long for the days when we fell short of winning the fifty-yard dash on field day or misspelled the word *propaganda* at the annual spelling bee. Those innocent failures seemed monumental at the time, but as we age, they slip gracefully into the background of our memory. As we get bigger, they are overshadowed by bigger failures. Addictions. Broken relationships. Shattered marriages. Crumbling businesses.

Living with failure is often more than we can humanly take. The feelings of shame, guilt, and sorrow can have crippling effects on our lives. Divorce and suicide ravage our culture. Doctors' offices are filled with patients suffering from anxiety, stress, and depression. We seek to be an ideal that we can't quite live up to—and the failure to do so is killing us.

No one knows failure better than Peter. Jesus nicknamed him "the Rock," but Satan sifted and winnowed his faith till he was poured out like sand, leaving him all but decimated. Still, something tremendous happened to Peter on that evening of his greatest failure: His self-confidence, self-reliance, and stubborn self-will died. He was left broken and hollow. But he was saved by the look. The look that said he was forgiven. The look that said he was still God's child.

Unlike Judas, Peter, stripped of all that he thought he was, clung to that look, that truth. In the midst of his desperation, he claimed the truth of God's mercy and forgiveness and chose life. Judas chose death.

Our failures can force us to collapse inward in constant judgment of ourselves, or they can cause us to look upward into the face of forgiveness. The choice is ours. We can stay in a crumpled heap on the ground; or like Peter, no matter what pain we know the sunrise will bring, we can push ourselves to our feet and claim Christ's promises of hope, forgiveness, and eternal life.

Chapter Ten

The Betrayal

Early in the morning, all the chief priests and the elders of the people came to the decision to put Jesus to death. They bound him, led him away and handed him over to Pilate, the governor.

When Judas, who had betrayed him, saw that Jesus was condemned, he was seized with remorse and returned the thirty silver coins to the chief priests and the elders. "I have sinned," he said, "for I have betrayed innocent blood."

"What is that to us?" they replied. "That's your responsibility."

So Judas threw the money into the temple and left. Then he went away and hanged himself.

Matthew 27:1–5

The Betrayal

Recklessly, Judas falls out into the temple courtyard and through the gate. Satan has relentlessly pummeled his faith, shattering his heart and leaving him utterly alone. There remains but a tiny grain of faith that Satan has not yet winnowed, spilling over now in overwhelming remorse. Judas glances down at the hands that have betrayed Innocence, guilty tears blurring his vision. His gnarled face looks skyward, grief and torment shredding his soul. Like a burning torch among sheaves of wheat, this all-consuming agony sets his body aflame, sending him reeling like a drunkard through the streets. Ripping his clothing in anguish, he runs frantically around the temple corner, falling in a crumpled heap onto a peddler's cart.

"Look what you've done!" the peddler shouts.

Scrambling to his feet, Judas spots a length of rope hanging from the peddler's donkey. One swift move and he's running again. Running from what he has done.

The psalmist's words stab his heart: "If you, O Lord, kept a record of sins, who could stand? But with you there is forgiveness." But Judas shakes his head. There could be no forgiveness for what he has done. For him, there is no mercy. No grace. No pardon. There is only this chasm of deafening silence.

The events of only a few hours ago fire an arsenal of shame against his conscience...

It was dark when he fled the upper room, drops of cold perspiration forming on his upper lip, twisted thoughts of greatness inflaming his pride. The chief priests were expecting him; they'd kept a Roman contingent on call. Dressed in short, pleated tunics, a throng of armed soldiers moved out on their command, following

Judas. Pleased, the priests drank to the good fortune of having Judas within their ranks as he led the soldiers out the city gate, through the winding streets, into the Valley of Kidron, and up the gentle slope that leads to Gethsemane.

Judas was the only apostle to come from Kerioth, a region of Judea in the southern province of Palestine. The other eleven were from Galilee, the most northerly province.

He could have told the soldiers where to find Jesus, but then he would have missed seeing the look of betrayal on his teacher's face. An identifying kiss to the cheek would provide the ultimate drama, the ultimate revenge. His heart fluttered nervously as he envisioned Jesus' pain-stricken face as he was dragged away. Rivulets of sweat raced down his face and neck, soaking into the collar of his robe. Holding up his hand to stop the contingent behind him, he wiped the moisture from his face, straining his puffy, red-tired eyes to see into the thicket of olive trees. Shards of moonlight spilled into the garden as he focused on a figure in white. Just as he had suspected: Jesus had come here to pray. Judas smiled smugly, anticipating the surprise.

Adrenaline boiled in his veins, and his face stung with blood as he sicked the hounds of hell onto their prey. Practically foaming at the mouth, he ran to keep up with his evil comrades, eager to move in for the kill. The mongrels surrounded Jesus as the bewildered Peter, James, and John leaped to their feet. Hungry for revenge, Judas forced his way through the middle of the snarling pack, his crooked smile betraying the evil in his heart.

Slithering forward, Judas grabbed Jesus' shoulders and looked into eyes that still offered friendship… grace…love. "Greetings, Rabbi!" he said with perverted satisfaction, leaving a kiss upon the Master's cheek.

"Friend," Jesus responded, "do what you came for."

The unleashed animals lunged forward. Judas hadn't counted on Peter's sword-wielding antics, but what folly they added to the event! And the view of the three terrified apostles stumbling blindly into the night—no longer so confident, so smug, so mighty— was truly priceless.

"Who holds the power now, you cowards?" he seethed.

He was knocked to the ground and nearly trampled as the drooling, yapping curs dragged away their prize. Giddy and brimming with disdain, Judas pushed himself up from the ground, wiping his hands clean. The sound of a snapping twig spun him round on his feet. His heart raced; his breath came in short spurts. Perspiration poured down his body.

He was alone.

Then another noise from deep inside the olive grove sent him fleeing from the *garden*...

The weight of his crime speeds his flight as he sprints out of town, away from the temple. Away from the priests. Away from the gruesome reality. When had he allowed Satan's poison to subtly seep into his bloodstream? When had the sifting of his faith begun?

When Jesus had said, "Follow me," he had. In the beginning he had been as devoted and affectionate a follower as the other men. However, he was the only disciple from Kerioth, a region of Judea; the rest had come from Galilee, making him instantly feel like the outsider. They could see he was gifted, and his confidence and abilities had enabled him to act as treasurer of the group. But even as treasurer he had never been part of Jesus' inner circle. Peter, James, and John had those positions. How could he hold a significant office yet not be part of this tight circle of friends?

The words of Jesus resound through his head: "Have I not chosen you, the Twelve? Yet one of you is a devil!" He had known! Long before Judas began contemplating betrayal, Jesus had known what was simmering beneath the surface. He could read it in the restlessness. The prayerlessness. The stubbornness. The little jealousies, resentments, and quarrels with

John 13:21–22: "After he had said this, Jesus was troubled in spirit and testified, *I tell you the truth, one of you is going to betray me.*' His disciples stared at one another, at a loss to know which of them he meant." At this time, even Judas was unaware that he would be the one to betray Jesus.

the other disciples. The creeping anger that would strike at a moment's notice with a keen, sharp blade. Though the others were unaware, Jesus had not missed his selfishness, masked as concerned interest and camouflaged by good works.

Now his sin plagues his soul as he runs faster and faster, blood pounding in his ears. He could still hardly believe Jesus' words at the Passover meal just last night.

He had been contemplating his treachery, when Jesus bent to wash his feet, looking at him, appealing to him as his friend and teacher. Then Jesus spoke the words that sent him bolting into the night alone: "One of you shall betray me."

"Is it I, Lord?"

"Is it I?"

"Am I the one?" Judas asked.

Jesus' reply was simple—a morsel of forgiveness held in the open palm of his hand.

"As you say."

It had been more than Judas could take.

It is more than he can take now. He runs wildly, lungs splintering with every stride.

Chapter Ten

For thirty pieces of silver he had betrayed innocent blood. The chief priests' words clang louder and louder with each step.

"That's your responsibility," they had sneered.

"That's *your* responsibility!"

"THAT'S YOUR RESPONSIBILITY!"

He cannot live with the responsibility.

The tree stands on a cliff just outside of town. His shaking hands fasten one end of the rope around an overhanging branch and hurriedly tie the other end to form a loop. His heart throbs as he slides the rope over his head, the words of Lamentations pricking his mind but too torturous, too sufferable to think upon: "Because of the Lord's great love we are not consumed, for his compassions never fail. They are new every morning." The anguish of betraying Jesus makes those words impossible for him to believe.

With one quick motion he tightens the noose around his neck and throws his body over the edge of the cliff.

The rope jerks tight.

A gentle *squeak, squeak, squeak* fills the air as his

body swings against the backdrop of the brilliant Galilean sky…alone.

Your Walk with Him

It's easy to discard Judas as a criminal, a villain, or a devil—to picture him on the FBI's "Most Wanted" list. But believing he was any of these things casts a shadow on the character and judgment of Jesus. The Bible tells us, "One of those days Jesus went out to a mountainside to pray, and spent the night praying to God. When morning came, he called his disciples to him and chose twelve of them, whom he also designated apostles" (Luke 6:12–13). Jesus' judgment was not shaky or questionable. He had spent an entire night in prayer with his Father. His thinking was clear; the Father's plan was laid out. Judas was not a traitor, thief, or criminal when he was chosen as one of the Twelve. He had looked like the other eleven men. He had heard the same messages. Witnessed the same miracles. Observed the same healings. He had followed God in the flesh for three and a half years.

But hearing, witnessing, and following don't make

a disciple. Judas was in the right company and was going through the right motions, but he wasn't walking with Jesus. Little bricks of resentment and stubbornness were laid one at a time, building a hard path between him and camaraderie with Jesus—each brick providing a steppingstone for Satan. It was Judas who laid those bricks. Not Jesus. His bitterness, anger, and jealousy mixed the mortar that formed his path of destruction. Satan gained his foothold and, step by devastating step, led Judas down a path of ugly mortar and broken brick, one that took him farther and farther away from Jesus.

It's easy to say the right things, associate with all the right people, and do the right activities, like going to church and even teaching Sunday school. It's amazingly easy to look like we're doing all the "right"-eous things. We're around God. We even say we love and follow God. But are we walking with him? Truly walking?

Or in the midst of all our upright living, are we slowly mixing mortar, preparing to lay our own paths of destruction?

Chapter Eleven

A Doubter's Faith

Now Thomas (called Didymus), one of the Twelve, was not with the disciples when Jesus came. So the other disciples told him, "We have seen the Lord!"

But he said to them, "Unless I see the nail marks in his hands and put my finger where the nails were, and put my hand into his side, I will not believe it."

A week later his disciples were in the house again, and Thomas was with them. Though the doors were locked, Jesus came and stood among them and said, *"Peace be with you!"* Then he said to Thomas, *"Put your finger here; see my hands. Reach out your hand and put it into my side. Stop doubting and believe."*

Thomas said to him, "My Lord and my God!"

Then Jesus told him, *"Because you have seen me, you have believed; blessed are those who have not seen and yet have believed."*

John 20:24–29

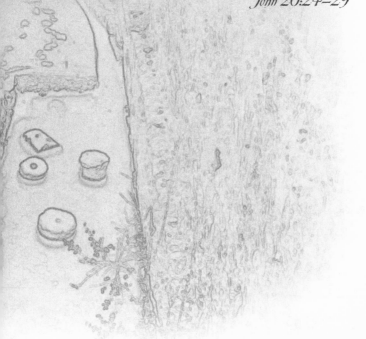

A Doubter's Faith

$\mathcal{F}or \; three \; days \; the$ apostles have lived in absolute terror of what they fear the Jewish leaders are doing: patiently waiting for them to surface, the way a spider waits for a fly to wing head-on into its web. So for three days they've cowered together in this home. Jumping at every noise. Flinching at every creak. All of them…except Thomas. He cannot bring himself to be with the other men. Each minute only heaps more agonizing blackness onto his depression, further widening his gully of fear and desperation.

Life has carried on for the rest of Jerusalem. Jesus died, and everyone went home. But life will never simply "carry on" for Thomas again. Thomas has always suffered from doubts and anxiety in the tedium and dailiness of living, but now that Jesus is dead, all hope seems to have died with him. For Thomas, this is the darkest night of his soul. He pulls a blanket of gloom further over his head, burrowing deeper and deeper into his wretched pit of despair.

Meanwhile, hour after excruciating hour has passed without a word spoken among the rest of the apostles. No words can possibly ease this yoke of unbearable suffering. If only they could turn back the clock, erase time. But time cannot be erased—it can only plod along at this torturous crawl, a deafening, unforgiving reminder of their guilt and cowardice.

Fearing for their own lives, they had all fled into the shadows after Jesus' capture. With the exception of John, they'd cowered in the darkness while the Romans nailed Jesus to the cross. *That cross!* When Jesus used to speak of his kingdom, none of them had ever pictured a *cross*. A kingdom is made up of a king and his royal court. There are chariots and white horses and a crown of gold. Not a crown of thorns! Not a whip with shards of stone! Not hammers! Not spikes! Not spears to pierce the king's side or angry Roman fists to pummel his face! When Jesus had spoken of his kingdom, they hadn't envisioned his tortured, bloody, flogged, beaten body stretched out on a *cross* while people mocked and cursed him. The kingdom they'd imagined didn't include a cross.

And now *that cross* has left them broken beyond human comprehension. They are unable to console or comfort one another. There is no balm for their wounded hearts. So they each suffer quietly, alone, their grief leaving them sick and tormented...until they hear the words that offer a glimpse of redemption.

"I have seen the Lord!"

Breathlessly, Mary Magdalene rushes into the home with the amazing news. Peter and John bolt from the house, leaving the others to wait. The seconds creep by as years before Peter and John return.

"The tomb is empty!" Peter shouts.

Not sure whether they're frightened or excited, the

apostles and other followers begin to nervously pray. Then, out of nowhere, Jesus appears in the center of them.

Jesus! Together the disciples experience the unimaginable joy of their risen Christ. Together they laugh and cry. And together they hold on to one another in dizzying emotion. All…except Thomas. Buried beneath his hopelessness, he misses the return of the Savior. He misses the tear-filled fellowship among his brothers. He misses the indescribable worship in praise of Christ's presence. His continual doubts, fears, frustrations, and disappointments have caused him to miss the extraordinary vision of the risen Lord, to miss his wonderful "Peace be with you!" But there is no peace for Thomas. There is only the falling debris of angst and fear from a disillusioned heart.

Some traditions have placed Thomas's missionary journeys in India. Others have placed his work farther east.

Thomas had come to trust his fellow disciples as truthful, honorable men. They'd worked for three and a half years to earn that trust—some working harder than others to win him over. But now, as they share with him the living reason for their rejoicing, the resurrected cause for their jubilation, Thomas staunchly and categorically refuses to believe them. Brow furrowed and head emphatically shaking, Thomas pours cold water on the apostles' impassioned belief.

"Unless I see the nail marks in his hands and put my finger where the nails were, and put my hand into his side, I will not believe it," he says.

In one skeptical breath he has managed to insult not only the apostles but also Jesus himself. But there remains the slightest prayer in Thomas's remark. *Unless.* It is a pleading prayer that God will restore his hope. Will ease his doubting heart.

Days plod along, but God does not answer Thomas's prayer. He spirals farther into dejection, his hopes and dreams nailed forever to that God-forsaken cross. Day after day the apostles invite him to join them in the house, but he adamantly refuses until…the seventh day. Finally the apostles break through Thomas's mulish stubbornness, and he walks wearily along with them to the house. Dragging his melancholy feet. Wringing his pessimistic hands.

He sits slumped in the corner while the others sing songs of praise and worship to their risen King. Even his downcast spirit cannot spoil their celebration. He slinks farther and farther into the woodwork. Suddenly, Jesus appears—in spite of bolted doors— right in the middle of the room. At least it *looks* like Jesus. But Thomas isn't sure. No, it can't be!

"Peace be with you!"

The voice sounds vaguely like Jesus', but lots of people can sound like someone else.

Jesus walks past his followers and approaches the crouching Thomas. He caresses his faithless, doubting child with words Thomas knows so well.

"Put your finger here; see my hands."

Thomas begins to tremble.

"Reach out your hand and put it into my side."

Reborn hope streams in tears down Thomas's face.

"Stop doubting and believe."

Thomas falls to the floor in a shaking heap at the scarred feet of his Savior. In one beautifully crafted testimony, his heart cries out, "My Lord and my God!" He has cast off skepticism. He has cast off stubbornness. He has cast off doubt.

Jesus speaks to his apostle—this one constantly plagued with unbelief—with words that will forever change his life: "Because you have seen me, you have believed; blessed are those who have not seen and yet have believed."

Thomas stands, his faith renewed. His spirit redeemed. His hope reclaimed. He will leave this place and find those who are bogged down in the dailiness of life. Those who can no

One tradition claims that while Thomas knelt praying, he died a martyr's death from a shower of arrows. Others claim he died from being thrust through with a spear.

longer find hope in the monotony of each day. He will tell them about his risen Lord. He will tell them that life had all but smothered him until Jesus walked through the locked door of his soul. He will tell them that his dreams were buried under an avalanche of dejection until Jesus showed him his scars.

And he will tell them that his life was smoldering beneath an ash heap of doubt until Jesus rose from the grave.

Your Walk with Him

Throughout history he's been known simply as "Doubting Thomas." But that name doesn't seem to say quite enough about such a melancholy, skeptical, gloomy soul. We all know people like Thomas. We've all seen that constant sour expression on the face of that person we work with. We've all cringed at seeing those same slumped shoulders on that glum family member. We've all rolled our eyes hearing that persistent murmur of catastrophe beneath a friend's breath. One can only take so much of the "glass-is-practically-empty" mind-set before moving on to sunnier friends. But Jesus *called* Thomas to be one of the Twelve. He saw something in Thomas that could minister to others. That could minister to us.

What was it that turned Thomas into such a faithless doubter? What turns us into such hard-to-be-with skeptics? Perhaps it was an abusive mother. Maybe an alcoholic father. It could have been a lengthy illness that finally claimed the life of a beloved friend. Pain plus the smallest disappointments begin to accumulate, and before we know it, we're buried beneath a mountain of doubt.

But whatever that mountain consists of, Jesus knows. He knows the hurt. He knows the disappointment. He also knows that like Thomas, our outlook will never change until we unquestionably, undeniably, indisputably put our faith in him. Just like Thomas, we have to make the effort to reprogram our negative attitudes and behavior.

Doubting in and of itself isn't the problem. Doubts can actually bring us closer to Jesus by increasing our faith. But the lost job, the chemotherapy, the infertility, the bankruptcy, the home that won't sell, the accident, the medical prognosis, the death of a child, the death of a marriage can all pack a heavy load of disappointment and disillusionment into our cannon of doubt. Unbelievably, these pains and losses *can* cause us to seek Christ in a greater way. Or they can smother our one struggling seedling of hope with a compost pile of dejection, dread, and depression.

Like Thomas, we can make doubt and frustration a way of life. Words like "This is never going to work," "Oh, brother," or "I'll believe it when I see it" can easily become part of our lifestyle if we don't make the effort to change. But it's so hard to be positive in this world of pedophiles, murderers, rapists, smarmy politicians, crooked evangelists, corrupt businessmen, and dysfunctional homes. We say it was *easier* for Thomas. He *saw* the scars. He could *see* the reason for hope. *Seeing* increased his faith.

Apparently, faith didn't come easily for Thomas. Perhaps he struggled daily to overcome a pain in his past. Daily disillusionment may have wound snake-like through his core. Hardening his disposition. Darkening his point of view.

Belief doesn't come easily for many of us. Sometimes we can barely muster enough faith to get out of bed in the morning. At one time our faith may have shone brilliantly; but as we've gotten older, per-haps the shine has grown dull, making it harder and harder to believe in anything or anyone. Maybe, like Thomas, our faith has been riddled with a constant shellfire of disappointment, skepticism, and doubt.

We need to learn what Thomas finally learned: that Jesus hung on the cross for our disappointments. He revealed his scars for our skepticism. And he rose from the dead for our doubts.

"Stop doubting and believe."

Chapter Twelve

The Cup

Then James and John, the sons of Zebedee, came to him. "Teacher," they said, "we want you to do for us whatever we ask."

"What do you want me to do for you?" he asked.

They replied, "Let one of us sit at your right and the other at your left in your glory."

"You don't know what you are asking," Jesus said. *"Can you drink the cup I drink or be baptized with the baptism I am baptized with?"*

"We can," they answered.

Jesus said to them, *"You will drink the cup I drink and be baptized with the baptism I am baptized with, but to sit at my right or left is not for me to grant. These places belong to those for whom they have been prepared."*

When the ten heard about this, they became indignant with James and John. Jesus called them together and said, *"You know that those who are regarded as rulers of the Gentiles lord it over them, and their high officials exercise authority over* them. Not so with you. Instead, whoever wants to become great among you must be your servant, and whoever wants to be first must be slave of all. For even the Son of Man did not come to be served, but to serve, and to give his life as a ransom for many."

Mark 10:35–45

The Cup

It is a day like so many others James has known—the sun blazing golden yellow, baking heat into the surrounding hills; the waters of the sea glistening, sending shimmering glints of silver beneath the throbbing light; the air clean, crisp, as if freshly washed. James draws the air deep into his lungs as he heads out once again to tell others about the kingdom of God.

The opposition, he knows, is growing. Increasingly embittered and fearful, King Herod and the Roman government have been plotting how to extinguish the expansion of any "kingdom" that threatens their power. In the eleven years since the crucifixion of Jesus, the name of Christ has continued to be spoken, and the movement of his followers has not been quashed as the Romans had hoped; it has only gained momentum. Now the Roman rulers have begun to despise the names of Jesus' apostles. These followers are bold. Aggressive. Fearless in getting Christ's message out to the people.

Word is dispatched to a small Roman contingent to seize James, one of the loudest and boldest of the apostles, and to swiftly kill him. As the soldiers drag him through the streets, James anticipates the taste of the cup he will momentarily drink—the cup Jesus had asked him about. The cup of suffering. The cup of agony. As the Romans kick and beat him, James takes the cup and drinks of his destiny—a destiny unlike anything he could have ever imagined...

Even as a child James knew he was destined for greatness. As a youngster, his competitiveness set him apart from other children his age. Working with his father and brother on the fishing boats was only a steppingstone to the cushioned life he envisioned for himself. One day, he would take over his father's business and speedily turn it into the most successful and lucrative in the fishing industry. Servants would shuffle in and out of rooms to attend him. His wife would wear

In A.D. 44 James was the first apostle martyred for his faith.

only the finest garments. His sons would attend the best schools. These were lofty and ambitious goals, to be sure, but nothing his parents had not already instilled in him.

His mother, Salome, was accustomed to getting what she wanted: the finest clothing her husband's earnings could afford, premium linens, choice fruits and vegetables. She had a reputation in town for being demanding, and she unfailingly lived up to it. If her husband seemed to be unbending toward a desire or wish, she would simply set her chin and settle in for a lengthy, scowling bout of silence.

James and his younger brother, John, learned early from their mother that opportunity may strike only once and that their best interests should be considered first when any such prospect arose. She told them countless times: "There's only one way to get ahead in this world, and that is through ambition, drive, and looking out for number one." To aspire to anything less would have been disgraceful and a terrible disappointment to their mother.

When Jesus first asked James and John to follow him, Salome heartily approved. After all, there was talk that Jesus was the long-awaited Messiah. Early involvement in his ministry would give her sons a leg up in the kingdom-building process. With their motivation, abilities, and self-confidence, they could even be second and third in rank behind Jesus. Fishing had been very good to their family, but James and John had always shown potential to be so much more than simple fishermen. Following Jesus could be very good for their careers, very good indeed! And not only would she be the wife of Zebedee; she would be the mother of James and John, "leaders of the kingdom."

Growing up, James had eagerly devoured his mother's teachings and lived them out at school, in the synagogue,

The Cup

and on the boat. Be bold. Be aggressive. Be strong. Seek power, position, wealth. When Jesus asked James to follow him, James saw a ladder of social prestige, religious influence, and financial ease—and James intended to grab hold of that ladder and *climb*.

But to ensure his position within Christ's kingdom, James knew he would have to act quickly, before the other men. Jesus had already made Peter leader of the Twelve. James didn't mind the choice nearly as much as the thought that Jesus hadn't even *considered* him for the role—a role he was much more capable of handling. Perhaps Jesus hadn't considered him for the leadership position because he hadn't made it clear that he was willing to assume the responsibility. This time, James would not be so foolish. He would make his request clear to Jesus.

James and John waited until the other men were far from earshot before approaching Jesus. This was a business matter, and business was always conducted privately and professionally. Clearing his throat, James boldly asked, "Lord, would you give John and I positions at your right and left side when we come into the kingdom?"

Chapter Twelve

Jesus stared into James's deep black eyes, piercing the empty contours of his heart. James held his gaze—something he had learned from his mother—and stood firm.

"You don't know what you are asking," Jesus steadily replied. "Can you drink the cup I drink or be baptized with the baptism I am baptized with?"

Anyone who had ever known James knew that no task was too large and no assignment too demanding for him to tackle. Drinking from a cup and being baptized were much simpler charges than James had expected. "We can," he answered, full of brazen confidence.

He didn't know what he was saying. He didn't know that Jesus was preparing for a

One tradition maintains that when James was to be executed, one of the Roman guards who led him to his death was so moved that he confessed to being a Christian too. Legend has it that James turned to him, said, "Peace be to thee, brother," and kissed him—and the two men were beheaded together.

kingdom not of this world. He thought Christ was preparing for an *earthly* kingdom—one of greatness, beauty, majesty. He never imagined that suffering, pain, or death would be a part of that magnificent reign.

But he would soon realize the insignificance of his present dreams when Christ took hold of the cup handed to him by the Father. When Jesus was captured in Gethsemane, James ran from the terrifying cup. When the Romans nailed Jesus to the cross, James hid from the deadly cup. When they rolled the stone in front of the tomb, James cowered in the shadows, despondent over the life-defeating power of the cup. As he wept, his face in his hands, he knew as Jesus had, that he was not able to drink of that same *cup*...

But today, as the Romans force him to his knees before an executioner's block, James would drink. He would drink boldly of the cup from which Christ drank. Once, it had been his ambition to have a position of prominence in Christ's kingdom. To lord his power over others. To serve his own greater end. To have others serve him. But James's ambitions had changed to those of Christ. He exercised power, but only in his own life as he served those around him. The road he'd sought to prominence and fame had ended at the resurrection. When Christ rose from the grave, James faithfully walked a new road—the road of servanthood.

And now, kneeling at the end of that road, he reaches toward heaven, takes hold of the cup…and drinks.

Your Walk with Him

Many of us suffer from the terminal disease of "I want." No matter what we have, it's never enough. There's always something that's newer, faster, and better; and we want it. But the more we worry about getting what we want, the less time we seem to have to do anything else. We'd like to try, as Jesus said, "to give our lives," but honestly, there's just not enough time! We're driven and motivated, yes, but often it's toward all the wrong things.

James was driven. He was by far the most ambitious of the apostles. Power meant a lot to James. Imagine his astonishment when Jesus said, "Whoever wants to become great among you must be your servant, and whoever wants to be first must be slave of all. For even the Son of Man did not come to be served, but to serve, and to give his life as a ransom for many." James must have thought, *Who has ever been successful by serving?*

But God's idea of success and our idea of success are often polar opposites. God's idea of success is to faithfully carry out his will in our lives. God's idea of power is to use the power we have to help and serve the people around us. His idea of prominence is to give ourselves as servants to others. God wants us to walk the road of servanthood, but we want to walk the road of power, prestige, and acquisition. Our plans for great job promotions, enormous wealth, and positions of greatness do not include being anybody's servant.

James's ambitions and drives would change. His mother's would also change. In Scripture we see that Salome was at the cross (Mark 15:40–41) and at the tomb to anoint Jesus' body with spices (Mark 16:1). She, too, was walking as a servant—giving of herself even in Jesus' final moments on earth and serving him in death.

If we are willing, like James and his mother, God will change our motivations and desires to match his. But what if God's plan isn't as exciting as our own? Jesus said in John 10:10, "I have come that they may have life, and have it to the full." Jesus wanted James to have a full life. But James first had to relinquish the things that were a hindrance to that life: his hunger for power, wealth, and prestige. In and of themselves, those things are not bad commodities; but when they're not used for God and his greater good, they can lead us away from him, not toward him.

We can cinch tight the strings around our sack of goals, plans, and ambitions and forge ahead down our own road to success, or we can empty that sack and let God fill it with his overwhelming abundance. We can *live* the full life of which Jesus spoke even when we don't *have* everything we want. And a full life in Christ is better than a sack full of clunky ambition and desires any day.

Jesus did many other miraculous signs in the presence of his disciples, which are not recorded in this book. But these are written that you may believe that Jesus is the Christ, the Son of God, and that by believing you may have life in his name.

John 20:30–31